CONTENTS

HISTORY OF THE DEPARTMENT

MAPS

ANCIENT NEAR EASTERN ANTIQUITIES

MESOPOTAMIA

IRAN

LEVANT AND
PRE-ISLAMIC ARABIA

ISLAMIC ANTIQUITIES

The Louvre

Near Eastern Antiquities

Annie Caubet
and Marthe Bernus-Taylor

EDITIONS
SCALA

Réunion des musées nationaux

© 1991 Scala Publications Ltd.
Published by Éditions Scala
14 bis, rue Berbier du Mets - 75013 Paris

Cover : *The official Ebih-Il*

HISTORY
OF THE DEPARTMENT

THE ANCIENT NEAR EAST

The Department of Near Eastern Antiquities is the latest department to have been founded at the Louvre; it was established officially only in 1881. The large winged genii from Khorsabad, however, were on view to the Parisian public from 1847 in the "Assyrian Museum"; the faded inscription is still visible on the pink marble lintel over a small door in the north-east corner of the Cour Carrée at the Louvre.

Today, the department is devoted to the ancient civilizations of the Near and Middle East, beginning with the earliest Neolithic villages of the 8th millennium BC and ending with Islam, which is the responsibility of a separate section of the department. The collections are drawn from an area that extends from North Africa in the west to India in the east; the largest part of the collections, however, comes from Mesopotamia, Iran and the Levant.

The size and diversity of these civilizations should not hide the fact that they indubitably each form part of a greater whole, with common characteristics that persist through time and space. The most obvious of these is language: Akkadian, Phoenician, Aramaic and Arabic all belong to the Semitic group; languages of this group have been spoken from the 3rd millennium BC to the present day.

Gate of the palace of King Sargon II of Assyria in Khorsabad (8th century BC). Reconstruction suggested by the excavator, Victor Place, in Ninive et l'Assyrie, Paris, Imprimerie Impériale, 3 vols, 1867-1870.

Other common factors are the landscape and climate and the living conditions imposed by these. The Fertile Crescent describes an enormous arc connecting Mesopotamia to the shores of the Mediterranean. The domestication of plants and animals living in this area in a wild state enabled man to master his environment and establish the first sedentary villages at the beginning of the Neolithic period in the 7th and 6th millennia BC. The next stage was the development from village to city, a true "urban revolution" which came about during the 5th and 4th millennia. The first urban civilizations came into being in the great river valleys irrigated by the Nile, the Tigris, the Euphrates and the Indus. The birth of a complex economy entailed the application of tools for accounting. Thus, around 3300-3000 BC, writing, the greatest contribution made by Mesopotamia to the modern world, came into being.

It is by means of writing that the civilization evolved to which we in the West in the 20th century are doubly heir: via the Biblical tradition and via Greece. Following the period of Alexander the Great, the East from the Mediterranean to India was hellenized, while retaining a part of its ancient heritage which it bequeathed to such intellectuals of mixed culture as Flavius Josephus, Berossus and Lucian of Samosata.

The history of the collections of the department is bound up with that of Near Eastern archaeology. The Louvre has been associated from the beginning with most of the important French excavations in the Near East: indeed, it could be said to have instigated them. The first investigations were carried out by diplomats posted to various parts of what was then the Ottoman Empire. Scientific expeditions became fashionable after Napoleon's expedition to Egypt in 1789, when French diplomats in the Near East were asked to write reports on the geography, the manners, the botanical, mineralogical and zoological resources and the antiquities in their areas. They wanted to find evidence of the Assyrians, who were then known only through the Bible. Paul-Emile Botta (1802-1870), then French consul in Mosul, was looking for Nineveh when he started to excavate the ruins of Khorsabad in 1842; although he did not find Nineveh, he had the good fortune to discover the palace built by Sargon II, King of Assyria in the 8th century BC. Only a little later, his British colleague Austen Henry Layard found fame by identifying the ruins of Nineveh near Mosul. Botta, accompanied by Eugene Flandin, a draughtsman, excavated the central part of the Palace of Sargon; the halls had walls of unbaked mudbrick faced with orthostats carved with reliefs. Several hundred metres of reliefs were drawn *in situ*, and the inscriptions were copied. A selection of the best-preserved reliefs were then taken down and sent to France. They were shipped down the Tigris on rafts, the only means of river transport capable of taking their weight (the heaviest, a bull, weighed 30 tons), and then sent from Basra to Marseilles, circumnavigating Africa — the Suez Canal had not yet been excavated. The works of art shipped to France by Botta arrived without impediment at the Louvre, where the first "Assyrian Museum" was opened in 1847, less than five years after their discovery.

Fate was not so kind to Botta's successor at Khorsabad. Victor Place (1818-1875) excavated the site from 1852 to 1854, assisted by F. Thomas, an architect and G. Trenchard, one of the first archaeological photographers. The rafts of this expedition were attacked and sunk by Bedouin as they floated down the Tigris to Basra carrying all Place's notes as well as several reliefs, including one of a winged bull.

Does the Bible tell the truth? This question, which bears on the literal truth of all ancient sources, is parallelled by that in the mind of Schliemann, who travelled all over Greece looking for evidence of the War of Troy with a copy of Homer in his hand. The search for the answer to this question was one of the main motivations of the earliest explorations of the Holy Land. Ernest Renan, who had a profound knowledge of ancient Eastern languages, went to the Levant in 1860 with his sister Henriette, whose illness and death forced him to cut short his journey. He drew the inspiration for his *Life of Jesus*, which was published in 1863, from the observations he had made while in the Holy Land. It was one of the first attempts to portray the world of the Bible through a study of the society and environment of the area in modern times: "I was able to add a great source of enlightenment, actually seeing the places where the events took place, to the reading of texts... I traversed the Holy Land in all directions. I visited Jerusalem, Hebron and Samaria... The entire story, which seems from this distance to float in the clouds of an unreal world, thus took on a substance and solidity that astounded me. The striking accord of the texts with the places, the wonderful harmony of the ideal with the landscape in which it was framed were a revelation to me" (*Life of Jesus*, introduction). The Levantine collection at the Louvre began with antiquities that Ernest Renan brought back from Phoenicia — including the sarcophagus of Eshmunazar, the jewel of the Levantine collection. The collection was later enlarged by systematic campaigns of excavation at the sites of Byblos and Ugarit on the Mediterranean coast, and at Mari, capital of a kingdom of that name on the Euphrates. These excavations continued until the Second World War.

With the discovery of the Sumerians in 1877, a new page was turned in Near Eastern studies. Ernest de Sarzec, a diplomat posted in Basra, was alerted by one Mr Gilliotti, director of the Post Office in Baghdad. Returning from a tour of inspection of the telegraph lines, he had seen some statues which were strewn along the banks of the Shatt-al-Hai canal near the village of Telloh. When de Sarzec excavated the statues, it was established that they represented Gudea, a Sumerian prince of the city-state of Lagash in about 2310 BC. When they came to light, these statues provided the first evidence of a people whose memory, whose name even, had long since passed into oblivion. Yet it is to the Sumerians that we owe the very instrument of history, writing.

The investigation of the archaeology of Iran began somewhat later. In 1884, the engineer Marcel Dieulafoy and his intrepid wife Jeanne arrived at the site of Susa, where they proceeded to investigate the exposed levels, which included remains of enormous structures built by the Achaemenids. It is to them that the Louvre is indebted for the 7-meter-high capital of a column. In her journal, Jeanne Dieulafoy wrote: "...when I walk by these gigantic monoliths, I am filled with respect for the men who brought them from the Bakhtiari Mountains, the men who carved this black marble fine beyond compare and of unparalleled hardness, and then had the audacity to place colossi on column shafts 20 meters high..." (J. Dieulafoy, *A Suse: Journal de fouilles 1884-1886*, Paris, 1888).

Dieulafoy also discovered the renowned frieze of archers. The polychrome glazed bricks of which it consists had been dispersed: "...the frieze of archers grows. The lacunae are filled in: the torso which had eluded all our searching finally appeared. We despaired of finding one face — the face is always the preferred target of vandals. Since yesterday it has been represented by a glazed brick showing the lower lid of an eye drawn in full face, the nose, the cheek and the carefully curled green hair" (J. Dieulafoy, 1888).

After the First World War and the destruction of the Ottoman Empire, which had long ruled the Near East, the newly-formed Near Eastern governments established Departments of Antiquities and museums; this was the time in which scientific excavation was developing. The antiquities laws provided for the division of the finds of foreign archaeological missions. The Louvre was thus able to acquire a portion of the finds discovered by the French teams, which often included museum curators. Today, archaeological finds remain in the countries in which they are found, but the tradition of foreign excavations continues and the scientific staff of the Department of Near Eastern Antiquities still take part in excavations.

ISLAM

The vast area illustrated by the rich collections of objects from the Ancient Near East was conquered by the armies of Muhammad in the space of only a few years in the middle of the 6th century AD. Although the Near East formed the heartland of the mediaeval Muslim world, the lands dominated by Islam extended well beyond, from the Atlantic — Spain remained partly Muslim until 1492 — to the Philippines, from the Caucasus to Equatorial Africa. From the 7th to the 19th centuries the so-called "classic" Islamic territories, which extend from Spain to northern India, were the crucible of a brilliant and original civilization whose diversity, reflecting local traditions, enriched and reinforced its apparent unity.

If language appears to be the link that connects all of the Ancient Near East, the languages of the Islamic world are more diverse. Arabic is, of course, the language of the Quran, and religion is undoubtedly the strongest bond between all the peoples, so varied in race, tradition and language, who inhabit this world. Many languages are spoken besides Arabic, which is a Semitic language; of the others, the two most widespread are Persian, an Indo-European language, and Turkish, which belongs to the Uralo-Altaic group.

The collections of Islamic art in the Louvre are among the most important in the world, rivalling those in New York, London and Berlin. They cover a geographic area that extends from Spain to India, and include varying amounts of ceramics, brass wares, glass, wood and ivory carving, carpets and other textiles, miniatures and papyri. North Africa, however, is not represented at the Louvre; a department of the Musée des Arts Africains et Océaniens is consecrated to the Maghreb.

The history of the Islamic collections, unlike that of the Ancient Near Eastern collections, is not closely associated with the history of archaeology; except for the objects from the site of Susa, the Islamic collections represent rather a reflection of the history of taste and of the awakening of orientalism, thanks to the interest of several informed collectors at the end of the 19th century.

At this time the French royal collections were already in possession of some prestigious objects. The beautiful rock crystal ewer carved in an Egyptian workshop at the beginning of the 11th century and now exhibited in the Galerie d'Apollon was donated to the Abbey of Saint-Denis by the abbot and statesman Suger (1081-1151). Several jade cups enhanced with gold and precious stones, made in Turkey in the 16th century, were included in the inventories of Louis XIV, and the magnificent brass basin inlaid with silver and gold, a Syrian masterpiece of the beginning of the 14th century known as the "Baptistery of Saint Louis", comes from the treasury of the Sainte Chapelle of the Château de Vincennes. The Islamic section at the Louvre, however, was established in 1890. It came into being following the Sauvaget donation and thanks to the interest of two curators in the Department of Decorative Arts, Emile Molinier and Gaston

Migeon. In 1905 Migeon opened a gallery of "Muslim Art", the existence of which, in the prestigious setting of the Louvre, gave rise to donations of objects as well as of money. The Baroness Delort de Gléon, for example, bequeathed the remarkable collection of objects amassed by her husband in Egypt and the Near East to the Louvre in 1912, and also bequeathed a considerable sum for the establishment of a larger gallery; this gallery was opened in 1922 on the second floor of the Pavillon de l'Horloge and was named after the Baroness.

On the death of Gaston Migeon in 1923 the Islamic section was integrated into the Department of Asian Arts, still within the Department of Decorative Arts. After the Far Eastern collections were moved to the Musée Guimet, the Islamic section was attached to the Department of Near Eastern Antiquities in 1945.

The outstanding objects in the collection, which had been displayed for many years in the room at the centre of the Louvre, the former royal chapel, are now exhibited much more modestly; in 1933, however, a suite of 13 galleries devoted entirely to the Islamic collections was finally opened in the Richelieu wing.

It is not possible to list here all the benefactors who have contributed to the enrichment of the collections. There are a few, however, who deserve special mention. Georges Marteau was a collector of oriental miniature paintings. He was closely associated with Henri Vever, with whom he wrote the preface and commentary to the catalogue of the acclaimed exhibition of Persian miniatures in the Museum of the Decorative Arts in 1912. They both belonged to the circle of collectors of eclectic taste, like Siegfried Bing, Louis Gonse, Raymond Koechlin — one of the founders of the Friends of the Louvre and president of the Conseil Artistique des Musées — and Gaston Migeon, who were in at the very beginning of the fashion for orientalism and Japanese art. The legacy of Persian miniatures bequeathed by Georges Marteau in 1916 and that of metalwork of the 13th and 14th centuries and other diverse objects, bequeathed by Raymond Koechlin in 1932, added a large number of masterpieces to the collection. The Baroness Salomon de Rothschild left an assortment of objects — including metalwork from the Arabian Near East and Timurid Persia, sumptuous weapons from Mughal India and carpets from Isfahan — to the Louvre. Alphonse Kann, who was closely associated with Georges Salles, Director of the Louvre, gave the large plate made in Samarkand in the 10th century and decorated with the text of an adage, one of the best known examples of this series. Other objects were given by such well known people as Gaston Maspéro and Léon Schlumberger, scholars and archaeologists of note, René Chandon de Briailles, politician and historian of the Roman East, David David-Weill, one of the most prominent financiers of the 19th century, his son Jean David-Weill, curator of the Islamic section until 1969, whose modesty and learning were equalled only by his knowledge of the Arab world, Jeda Godard, wife of the architect and archaeologist André Godard, who was Director-General of the Archaeological Services in Iran from 1928 until 1960, and finally renowned antiquarians such as Nicolas Landau, Joseph Soustiel and his son Jean.

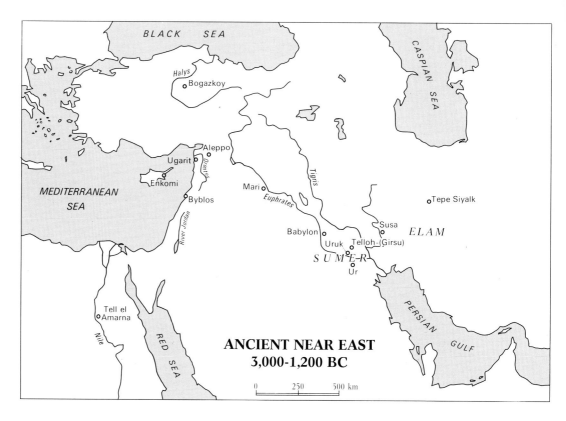

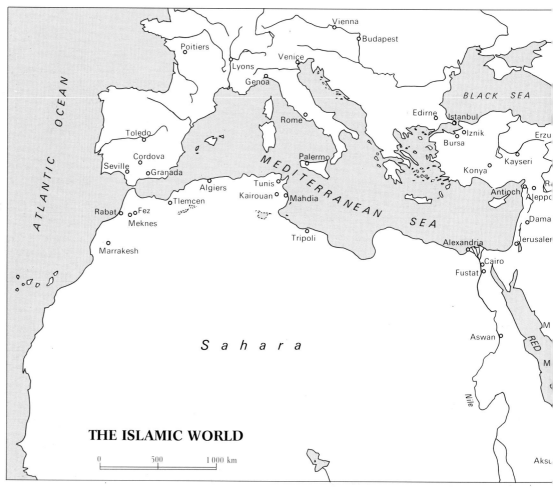

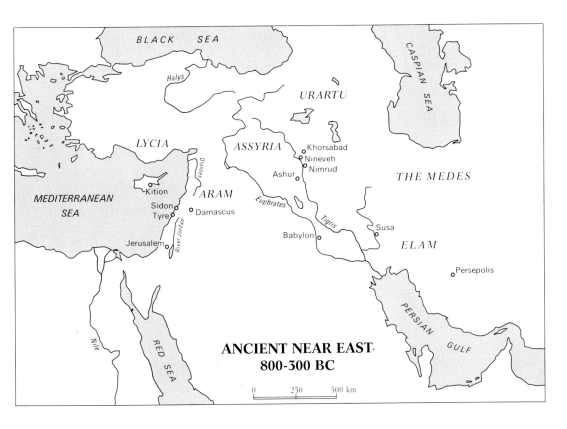

**ANCIENT NEAR EAST·
800-300 BC**

BLACK SEA

Halys

URARTU

LYCIA

ASSYRIA

Khorsabad
Nineveh
Ashur
Nimrud

THE MEDES

MEDITERRANEAN
SEA

Kition

ARAM

Orontes

Euphrates

Tigris

Sidon
Tyre

Damascus

River Jordan

Jerusalem

Babylon

Susa

ELAM

Persepolis

PERSIAN
GULF

CASPIAN SEA

Nile

RED SEA

0   250   500 km

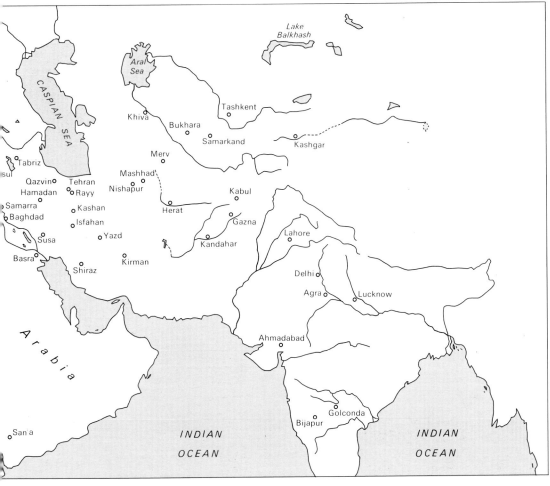

Lake
Balkhash

Aral
Sea

CASPIAN SEA

Tashkent

Khiva

Bukhara

Samarkand

Kashgar

Tabriz

Merv

sul

Qazvin

Mashhad

Hamadan

Tehran

Nishapur

Kabul

Rayy

Samarra

Kashan

Herat

Baghdad

Isfahan

Gazna

Susa

Yazd

Kandahar

Lahore

Basra

Kirman

Delhi

Shiraz

Arabia

Agra

Lucknow

Ahmadabad

Golconda

Bijapur

San'a

INDIAN
OCEAN

INDIAN
OCEAN

MESOPOTAMIA

The environment of the Fertile Crescent was conducive to the developments of the Neolithic: the beginnings of agriculture and animal husbandry entailed the evolution of the first sedentary villages. The beliefs connected with fertility and fecundity found their expression in deliberately stylized female figurines with ample proportions.

At the end of the 5th millennium large cities came into being. In the land of Sumer the organization of urban society was accompanied by new techniques: the beginning of monumental architecture and sculpture, the introduction of cylinder seals for the authentication of accounts and, finally, the invention of writing. Pictographic at first, it evolved towards the cuneiform, a term that derives from the appearance of the signs — they are wedge-shaped and wedge is *cuneus* in Latin.

A personage who has been designated the "priest-king" is often shown in early pictures. He appears in various aspects: in prayer, as a victorious warrior, as responsible for the abundance of the harvest and the fecundity of the flocks. It is perhaps within this context that some of the main Mesopotamian myths have their origin, like that of Gilgamesh, the legendary king who went in pursuit of immortality.

The development of writing and the appearance of historic inscriptions took place in the Early Dynastic period in Sumer between 2700 and 2350 BC. The land was then divided into small city-states each ruled by a prince *(ensi)*. The economy was based on agriculture and trade, in some cases over long distances; lapis lazuli ornaments link Mesopotamia with the Indus valley.

The unity of the land of Sumer is evident from the culture and the writings and from certain aspects of religious life. Within a common pantheon, each city claimed the protection of one or more divinities. When disputes over the frontiers between two city-states arose, the gods took part: the *Stele of the Vultures* commemorates the issue of the conflict between the state of Lagash and that of Umma; the victor was prince Eannatum of Lagash, who is seen at the head of his armies while the god Ningirsu assures the victory of those faithful to him.

King Sargon of Akkad ruled over populations that had settled in northern Mesopotamia speaking Akkadian, a Semitic language; it was he who unified the country. From his time on, Mesopotamian culture was bilingual, with Sumerian retained as the language of learning and religion while Akkadian became the language of communication and diplomacy.

The principal monuments of the kings of Akkad, originally consecrated in Mesopotamia, were found in Iran by the French archaeological mission excavating the site of the metropolis of Susa. They had been brought there as booty in the 12 century BC by Shutruk-Nahhunte, the Elamite conqueror. These monuments were carved in diorite, which had been brought back from the confines of India and which was reserved for the royal workshops. The victory stele of Naram-Sin, however, was made of sandstone. The sense of movement and space conveyed by the relief sculpture on this monument demonstrates the difference between the Sumerian tradition and the contribution of the people of Akkad.

The Akkadian Empire collapsed under the attacks of insubordinate mountain peoples who, in about 2200 BC, destroyed its unity. In the Sumerian south, the state of Lagash effectively recovered its autonomy under the authority of the dynasty of Prince Gudea in about 2130. This peaceful, religious monarch built temples to the gods of his city of Girsu, and most especially to Ningirsu, the city-god, sending to distant parts for the necessary materials. In these temples Gudea deposited statues of himself in eternal prayer, carved in the exotic diorite favoured by the great kings of Akkad.

*The prince
Ginak*
Early
Dynastic
Period c
2700-2600 BC
Gypsum
height 25.5 cm
Sumeria,
southern
Mesopotamia
Gift of the
Friends of the
Louvre, 1951
AO 20146

The Sumerian rulers of the Third Dynasty of Ur (2113-2206 BC) gradually re-unified the land, re-organizing it by careful administration, weaving an extended network of economic and political relations. It was a period of much intellectual, religious and artistic activity, signalled in architecture by the construction of ziggurats, tiered towers intended to facilitate the descent to earth of the gods at the times of the great festivals, such as that of the New Year. The First Dynasty of Babylon, under the impetus of Hammurabi (1792-1750 BC), whose diplomatic ability and shrewdness were equalled by his grasp of military matters, managed for a time to maintain this unity. The world owes a renowned monument, known as the *Code of Hammurabi* to this exceptional monarch; it is in fact a memorial to the glory of the "just" king, that his sense of justice and his wisdom might be known to posterity.

During the course of the second millennium BC, Mesopotamia again became fragmented. The centre and the south were dependent first on the Babylon dynasty and then on the Kassites. The north was divided between the Assyrians and the Kingdom of Mitanni, which extended to the Levant. Dynamic rulers, such as Shamshi-Adad I in the 19th century BC and Tukulti-Ninurta I in the 13th century, had elevated Assyria to the rank of the great powers. From the time of Ashurnasirpal II (833-859 BC) on, Assyria had an impact on the international stage. The Assyrian policy of conquest, based on an entirely modern administrative and military organization, is reflected on the walls of the palaces the Assyrians built in their successive capitals, Nimrud, Ashur, and Nineveh. Sargon II (721-705 BC) built a new city to which he gave his name, Dur-Sharrukin (modern Khorsabad). The Assyrian idea of kingship found expression in the decoration of the monuments, on which the role of the ever-present king as "vicar" is conveyed. P.E. Botta and V. Place brought back orthostats decorated with reliefs that show the king and his retinue performing various functions: at war, at the hunt and before the gods. The gates were guarded by human-headed winged bulls and by fabulous genii vanquishing lions, who have been wrongly identified as the hero Gilgamesh.

Assyrian might was cast down by the Medes, with whom the Babylonians had allied themselves. Babylonia underwent a brilliant revival during the 6th century BC, before the Achaemenid Persians unified the entire Near East. The Neo-Babylonian rulers built colossal structures in their capitals; these were characteristically faced with polychrome glazed bricks, an architectural technique that was to continue for a very long time in the Near East, for example in the tiled mosques of Isfahan and Istanbul.

The kings of Babylon, especially Nebuchadnezzar II (604-562 BC), pursued the politics of the Assyrians towards the Levant. Like the Assyrians, they were stigmatized by Biblical accounts that have preserved the appalling memory of conquests and deportations. Nevertheless, it is due to the Babylonian Exile that something of Mesopotamian culture is linked to the modern world through the Bible: thus the account of the flood was borrowed from a passage in the story of Gilgamesh and the tower of Babel preserves the memory of the ziggurats, or tiered towers. The confusion of tongues with which the overweening pride of the builders of the tower was punished reflects the polyglot culture of the Babylonians: their scribes were capable of writing in Sumerian, the language of learning that had remained in use since the 3rd millenium BC, in Aramaic, the Western Semitic language of the nomads of the Syrian plains who had gradually infiltrated Mesopotamia and finally, of course, in Babylonian, an evolved form of Akkadian.

The Persian conquest, which preceded that of Alexander, did not destroy the prosperity of Mesopotamia, which continued to prosper for much of the time that it was subject to the Seleucid Greeks and then to the Parthians. The concept of the Near East expanded to cover a vast area that included Persia and the Levant. The advent of Islam in AD 622 was to push back the limits even further.

Female figurine
c 5800-5500 BC
Alabaster inlayed with bitumen —
height 5.4 cm
Necropolis of Tell es-Sawwan,
central Mesopotamia
On deposit from the Baghdad Museum
since 1981
DAO 33

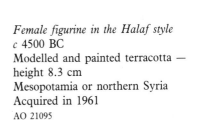

Female figurine in the Halaf style
c 4500 BC
Modelled and painted terracotta —
height 8.3 cm
Mesopotamia or northern Syria
Acquired in 1961
AO 21095

*Jar with geometric decoration
in the Halaf style*
c 4500 BC
Hand made terracotta — diameter 35.5 cm
Mesopotamia or northern Syria
Acquired in 1989
AO 29599

Bull in the Ubaid style
c 4000-3500 BC
Modelled and painted terracotta —
height 10.1 cm
Telloh, southern Mesopotamia
Excavated by A. Parrot 1931-32
AO 15310

Tablet with pictographic inscription
Protoliterate Period *c* 3300 BC
Unbaked clay incised with a reed pen —
height 7.2 cm
Southern Mesopotamia
Acquired in 1989
AO 29560

Naked praying chief
Protoliterate Period
c 3300 BC
Limestone —
height 25 cm
Southern Mesopotamia
Acquired before 1869
AO 5718

Pin decorated with two dancers
Protoliterate Period *c* 3000 BC
Copper — length 18.1 cm
Telloh, southern Mesopotamia
Excavated by H. de Genouillac 1930-1931
AO 14522

Cylinder seals
Mesopotamia
c 3300-2500 BC
Limestone, green stone and lapis lazuli
AO 6620, MNB 1906, AO 5371, AO 22299

The 4th millennium BC was the period of the first large cities, a true urban revolution accompanied by cultural advance: metallurgy developed on a grand scale, bringing in its wake the growth of long-distance trade, which in turn supplied the ores required by the metal industry. This trade and the growing complexity of the economy led in their turn to the invention of the means of accounting: the cylinder seal, with which deliveries of goods could be sealed to ensure their integrity and above all, writing, originally invented for the purpose of noting the nature and amount of a delivery.

Uruk style jar with scene in cattle shed
Protoliterate Period *c* 3300 BC
Limestone — height 24.5 cm
Acquired in 1924
AO 8842

Uruk style jar decorated with animals
Protoliterate Period *c* 3300 BC
Limestone — height 9.7 cm
Acquired in 1966
AO 21989

Colossal spearhead dedicated by Ur-Lugal,
King of Kish
Early Dynastic Period *c* 2600 BC
Telloh, ancient Girsu
Engraved copper — length 80 cm
Excavated by E. de Sarzec,
gift of Sultan Abdul Hamid, 1896
AO 2675

Dedication of a Sumerian chief to the god
Ningirsu, known as "the figure with
the feathers"
Early Dynastic Period *c* 2700-2600 BC
Limestone — height 18 cm
Telloh, ancient Girsu
Excavated by E. de Sarzec 1877-1898
AO 221

Figurine and foundation nail with the
name of Prince Ur-Nanshe of Lagash
Early Dynastic Period *c* 2494-2465 BC
Copper — height 14 cm
Telloh, ancient Girsu
Excavated by E. de Sarzec in 1881
AO 254

The official Ebih-Il
Early Dynastic Period *c* 2500 BC
Gypsum and lapis lazuli — height 52.5 cm
Mari, Middle Euphrates, Temple of Ishtar
Excavated by A. Parrot 1934-1935
AO 17551

Relief consecrated by Dudu,
priest of Ningirsu
Early Dynastic Period *c* 2450 BC
Bitumen — height 25 cm
Telloh, ancient Girsu
Excavated by E. de Sarzec 1877-1898
AO 2354

*Votive beard with dedication by a queen
of the city of Umma for the life of her
husband King Gishakidu*
Early Dynastic Period *c* 2400 BC
Gold — height 8.5 cm
Southern Mesopotamia
Acquired in 1937
AO 19225

*Mace-head inscribed in Sumerian with
the name of Mesilim, King of Kish, and
dedicated to the god Ningirsu*
Early Dynastic Period *c* 2550 BC
Limestone — height 19 cm
Telloh, ancient Girsu
Excavated by E. de Sarzec 1877-1898
AO 2349

*Jar dedicated by the prince Entemena
of Lagash to the god Ningirsu*
Early Dynastic Period *c* 2400 BC
Silver and copper — height 35 cm
Telloh, ancient Girsu
Excavated by E. de Sarzec,
gift of Sultan Abdul Hamid, 1896
AO 2674

Lamp in the form of a human-headed bull
Early Dynastic Period *c* 2500 BC
Gypsum — height 6 cm
Sumeria, southern Mesopotamia
Acquired in 1911
AO 5679

Ring with cloisonné decoration
Early Dynastic Period *c* 2400 BC
Gold and enamel — diameter 2.5 cm
Telloh, ancient Girsu
Bought by E. de Sarzec in 1881
AO 277

Priestess wearing a ceremonial headdress
Early Dynastic Period *c* 2500 BC
Gypsum — height 19.3 cm
Mari, Middle Euphrates, Temple of Ishtar
Excavated by A. Parrot 1934-1935
AO 18213

*Head of a bull with royal Sumerian
inscription, mount for a piece of furniture
or for a harp*
Early Dynastic Period *c* 2500-2400 BC
Copper — height 19 cm
Telloh, ancient Girsu
Excavated by E. de Sarzec,
gift of Sultan Abdul Hamid, 1896
AO 2676

Panel known as the "Standard of Mari"
Early Dynastic Period *c* 2500 BC
*Shell, limestone and bitumen —
width 72 cm
Mari, Middle Euphrates, Temple of Ishtar
Excavated by A. Parrot 1934-1935*
AO 19820

Worshipper dedicating a bull
Early Dynastic Period *c* 2500-2400 BC
Limestone — height 2.5 cm
Sumeria, southern Mesopotamia
Acquired in 1914
AO 6683

Pied Bull
Early Dynastic Period *c* 2500 BC
Bronze inlayed with silver — length 12 cm
Sumeria, southern Mesopotamia
Acquired c 1891
AO 2151

*Stele of the Vultures, dedicated by
Eannatum, prince of the state of Lagash,
in celebration of his victory over the city
of Umma*
Early Dynastic Period *c* 2450 BC
Limestone — height reconstructed
to 170 cm
Telloh, ancient Girsu
Excavated by E. de Sarzec in 1881 and
gift of the British
Museum
AO 50 + 2346

The French archaeologist Ernest de Sarzec discovered the civilization of Sumer while investigating
the site of Telloh, ancient Girsu, one of the cities of the
state of Lagash. The various aspects of Sumerian kingship are illustrated on stelae. Ur-nanshe, the founder of
the Lagash dynasty in about 2500 BC, is represented as
a builder-king, carrying a basket of bricks for the construction of a temple, whose inauguration he celebrates
with a banquet with his family. His grandson Eannatum
appears as a conquering king, triumphing over his ene-
mies with the help of Ningirsu, the god who protects
the city; his stele is known as the Stele of the Vultures
because it shows scavengers tearing vanquished soldiers
to pieces.

*Commemorative relief for the
construction of a religious building
by Ur-Nanshe, Prince of Lagash
and his family*
Early Dynastic Period
c 2494-245 BC
Limestone — height 40 cm
Telloh, ancient Girsu
Excavated by E. de Sarzec in 1888,
gift of the Ottoman
Government
AO 2344

The kings of Akkad succeeded in uniting Mesopotamia under their rule. Like the Sumerians, they had a policy of building and of commissioning commemorative monuments which are known thanks to the excavation of Susa: stelae and statues dedicated by Sargon of Akkad (2371-2316 BC), Manishtusu (2306-2292 BC) and Naram-Sin (2291-2255 BC) in various Mesopotamian cities were brought to Susa as booty by an Elamite king of the twelfth century BC.

Diorite, a very hard black stone imported from India and also used by Gudea, was first used in the royal sculpture workshops in the Akkadian period.

Statue of Manishtusu, King of Akkad
Akkadian period *c* 2250 BC
Diorite — height 88 cm
Susa, Iran, booty from Mesopotamia
Excavated by J. de Morgan in 1880
Sb 47 - Sb 9099

Victory Stele of Naram-Sin, King of Akkad, over the mountain-dwelling Lullubi
Akkadian period *c* 2230 BC
Pink sandstone — height 210 cm
Susa, Iran, booty from Mesopotamia
Excavated by J. de Morgan in 1890
Sb 4

Head of a statue of Prince Gudea
Neo-Sumerian Period *c* 2130 BC
Diorite — height 23 cm
Telloh, ancient Girsu
Excavated by E. de Sarzec, 1881
AO 13

Statue of Prince Gudea,
dedicated to Ningizzada
Neo-Sumerian
Period *c* 2130 BC
Diorite — height 45 cm
Telloh, ancient Girsu
Excavated by E. de Sarzec
(body) and Cros (head) in 1903
AO 3293

Gudea, a peaceful and religious prince who reigned around 2130 BC, dedicated himself to the embellishment of his city, Girsu, and the building of temples. He and his family placed statues of themselves, charged with perpetuating their prayers, before the gods of the city.

The Kingdom of Mari, founded in the 3rd millennium BC on the Euphrates, on the frontier between Syria and Mesopotamia, bears witness to the diffusion northwards of Sumerian civilization. The splendour of the palace of Mari, which was decorated with wall paintings before Mari was conquered and destroyed by Hammurabi of Babylon in about 1750 BC, was revealed by the excavations of André Parrot.

Foundation nail of Gudea, Prince of Lagash
Neo-Sumerian
Period *c* 2130 BC
Copper — height 29 cm
Telloh, ancient Girsu
Excavated by E. de Sarzec in 1889, gift of the Ottoman Government
AO 311

Princess of the family of Gudea, "the woman with the shawl"
Neo-Sumerian Period
c 2150-2130 BC
Steatite — height 17 cm
Telloh, ancient Girsu
Excavated by E. de Sarzec in 1880
AO 295

Lion, gate-guardian
Isin-Larsa Period *c* 1800 BC
Bronze — height 70 cm
Mari, Middle Euphrates,
Temple of Dagan
Excavated by A. Parrot in 1935
AO 19824

Investiture of the king by the goddess Ishtar
Isin-Larsa Period *c* 1800 BC
Wall painting — height 175 cm
Mari, Middle Euphrates,
palace of Zimri-Lim
Excavated by A. Parrot in 1935
AO 19825

Hammurabi praying before a sacred tree
(detail)
c 1750 BC
Bronze and gold — height 19.6 cm
Larsa, southern Mesopotamia
Acquired in 1931
AO 15704

Code of Hammurabi, King of Babylon
c 1750 BC
Diorite — height 225 cm
Susa, Iran, booty from Mesopotamia
Excavated by J. de Morgan in 1901
Sb 8

Babylonian monuments of the time of Hammurabi were discovered at Susa, where they formed part of the booty brought back from Mesopotamia. The crowned head is probably an effigy of Hammurabi himself; the features marked by the concerns of power express an ideal of wisdom and justice also manifest in the "Code", a collection of exemplary judgements enacted by the king in the course of his reign and inspired by Shamash, the sun god and god of justice.

Head of a king (Hammurabi?)
c 1750 BC
Diorite — height 15 cm
Susa, Iran, booty from Mesopotamia
Excavated by J. de Morgan in 1897
Sb 95

A sacred tree
(detail) *c* 1750 BC
Bronze and gold — height 22 cm
Larsa, southern Mesopotamia
Acquired in 1931
AO 15705

*Kudurru (charter for a grant of land) of
the Babylonian king Marduk-zakir-shumi*
Late Assyrian period *c* 850 BC
Limestone — height 32.5 cm
Uruk, southern Mesopotamia
Acquired in 1914
AO 6684

*Unfinished kudurru (Kassite charter for
grant of land)*
c 1200 BC
Limestone — height 54 cm
Susa, Iran, booty from Mesopotamia
Excavated by J. de Morgan in 1900
Sb 25

*Jar decorated with symbolic
motifs surrounding the goddess Ishtar*
c 1700 BC
Terracotta — height 20 cm
Babylonia
Acquired in 1913
AO 6501

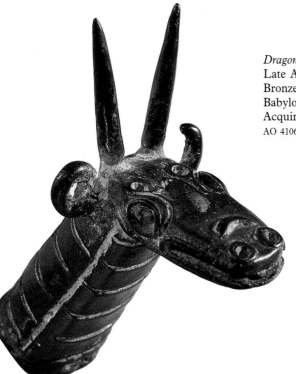

Dragon, symbol of the god Marduk
Late Assyrian period *c* 800-600 BC
Bronze — height 15 cm
Babylonia
Acquired *c* 1900
AO 4106

B abylon was the intellectual capital of Mesopotamia
for a very long time. At the time of the Kassite
domination, the rulers established their reigns with
grants of land guaranteed by charters in the form of stelae known as *kudurru*, and the royal scribes pursued a
policy of editing the great classical texts. The foremost
priests, scribes and diviners employed all over Mesopotamia, in Syria and by the Hittite court were trained in
Babylon, by the clergy of the god Marduk. Cuneiform
writing survived the conquests of Alexander; the scribes
who worked for the Seleucid kings transmitted some of
the science and religion of the Babylonians to the Greek
world.

Statuette of the goddess Ishtar
Hellenistic Period *c* 250 BC
Alabaster, gold, bronze and semi-
precious stones — height 25 cm
Babylonia
Gift of Pacifique Delaporte, 1866
AO 20127

S tarting from a small kingdom in northern Mesopotamia, the Assyrians carved out an empire that included the Levant at its largest expansion. Assyrian order
rested on an entirely new type of organization: the per-
manent army, the road system, the postal network, the
centralized administration supported by representatives
in the provinces, were all formidably efficient. In their
successive capitals, Ashur, Nimrud, Khorsabad, and
Nineveh, the Assyrian rulers built temples and palaces
whose painted and sculpted decoration reflected the royal
ideology: before his god, at war or at the hunt, the king
is the "vicar" of the god Ashur to his people.

*The demon Pazuzu, "king of the evil
spirits of the air"*
Late Assyrian Period c 800-700 BC
Bronze — height 14.5 cm
Assyria
Acquired in 1872
MNB 467

Winged Bull
Late Assyrian Period c 725 BC
Gypsum — maximum height 420 cm
Khorsabad, ancient Dur-Sharrukin,
Assyria, façade of the Palace of
King Sargon II
Excavated by P.-E. Botta 1842-1844
AO 19857

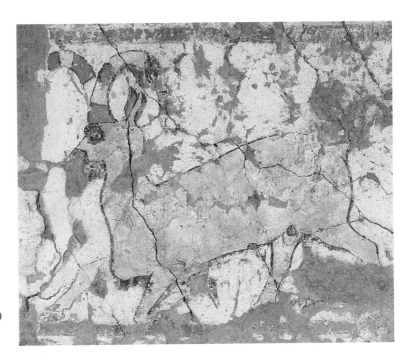

Blue goat
Late Assyrian Period *c* 800-700 BC
Wall Painting
Til Barsip, Assyrian palace
Excavated by F. Thureau-Dangin in 1930
AO 23010

Men with bows and arrows shooting birds
Late Assyrian Period *c* 725 BC
Gypsum — height 127 cm
Khorsabad, ancient Dur-Sharrukin,
Assyria, Palace of King Sargon II
Gift of Longeville, 1852
AO 19886

IRAN

Iran is a vast, high plateau, separated from Mesopotamia and from Central Asia by ranges of high mountains; in the south-west the fertile valleys of Elam open out onto the Mesopotamian plain, but in the east it is cut off by salt deserts. These natural frontiers have not, however, prevented contacts and trade with neighbouring countries; Iran was a staging post between the civilization of Mesopotamia and that of the Indus Valley, whose influence on the strong and original indigenous culture is discernible. The main centre of these meetings of cultures was the metropolis of Susa and its territory, Elam.

The history of the city of Susa was closely connected to that of Mesopotamia. Susa became a regional centre as the agricultural villages of the 5th and 4th millennia BC developed; valuable evidence of the first stages of the process of social, political and religious organization was preserved on the site of Susa. Stamp seals and then cylinder seals were used to seal despatches of merchandise, thus the first accounts took the form of hollow clay balls containing clay tokens. Later, when a sophisticated central administration developed at the end of the 4th millenium, inscribed clay tablets provided the earliest instruments of government, as they did in Mesopotamia.

During the 3rd and 2nd millennia BC, Susa and Elam oscillated between two worlds: at times the region was integrated into the Mesopotamian kingdoms, under the Dynasty of Akkad or the Third Dynasty of Ur; at times it was independent and nearly succeeded in conquering its conquerors, for example under the Median-Elamite dynasty. The 13th-century Elamite conqueror Shutruk-Nahhunte brought a prodigious amount of booty, taken from the temples of Babylonia, back to his capital at Susa: the Stele of Naram Sin, King of Akkad and the Code of Hammurabi were part of the spoils.

Superficially, Elamite civilization is very like that of Mesopotamia: the same brick architecture, the same types of temples and ziggurats, the same type of sculpture made of inlayed stone, the same use of clay tablets as writing material. These common characteristics, however, conceal profound differences - first of all the language, then the pantheon, whose divinities, manifestations of untamed natural forces, are those of a mountain people, quite different from the gods of the great riverine plains of Mesopotamia. This aspect is apparent in the quality and the enduring appeal of the animal art.

The development of metallurgy was one of the technological advances that, as mentioned above, accompanied the rise of cities. In this respect, Iran was undoubtedly in the forefront of the copper-working industry, thanks to the availability of ores and native copper that made possible the first working of copper by hammering as early as the 7th millennium BC. Urbanization accelerated the development of techniques, such as those of alloying and joining, and the use of precious metals. Rulers anxious to commemorate their reigns with prestigious monuments often chose to commission works of art in bronze, such as the statue of Queen Napirasu, wife of Untash-Napirisha, an Elamite king of the 12th century BC. The maquette in bronze of an open-air religious ceremony "to the rising sun" (Sit Shamsi) is another such work.

The vastness of the areas concerned did not impede trade, which took place over very long distances. The copper trade, indispensable to metal-working, is a case in point. Trade induced the growth of cultural and artistic contacts along the routes that connected eastern Iran, the southern parts of Central Asia, the Persian Gulf and Mesopotamia. The golden age of this trade was at the time when the civilization of Sumer and that of the Indus Valley (2500-2000 BC) were at their height. The peoples of eastern Iran specialized in the traffic

Mythological genius of the mountains
c 2200 BC
Limestone and chlorite, diadem made of meteoric iron —
height 11.7 cm
Eastern Iran
Acquired in 1961
AO 21104

in exotic stones, such as carnelian and lapis lazuli, imported from Afghanistan, and chlorite, a friable green stone used to make vessels with fine decoration and figurines. Composite sculptures using the contrasting colours of green chlorite, white limestone and red meteoric iron are reminiscent of colours and materials affected by Mesopotamian artists, whose work was also the inspiration for the dress of these figures. Susa was ideally placed to be a centre of the trade between East and West, a trade that encompassed raw materials as well as finished products, ideas, shapes and styles.

The Luristan bronzes demonstrate that objects of high artistic quality could be made on the Iranian plateau, far from any cities. They are the work of semi-nomadic mountain peoples, enriched by the international trade for which they furnished transport and probably also by some pillaging on the plains of Babylonia. These peoples were ruled by chiefs whose grandeur is displayed in the furnishings of their tombs: fine vessels and ceremonial weapons of which the earliest examples date to the end of the 3rd millenium BC; the height of this culture was attained in the first few centuries of the 1st millennium.

Horses were first bred for riding towards the end of the 2nd millennium BC; at this time horse trappings with extraordinary figured decoration began to appear in the tombs. The figure that constantly recurs is that of the master of the animals, a mythical being incarnating the wild forces of nature, which are embodied in exceptionally lively representations of animals.

Among these horsemen, there were two peoples who were destined to have a brilliant future: the Medes, who came from the area around Hamadan, and the Persians, who were settled in southern Iran in the region of Fars, which bears their name. They were united in the 6th century BC by Cyrus the Great, that wise and magnificent monarch whom the Greeks were forced to admire despite the threat to their civilization posed by the his armies. Under the rule of the dynasty of Darius the Achaemenid the Persians extended their empire, first to encompass the Iranian plateau, and then to the entire Near East, including the Levant and Anatolia. The Achaemenid rulers brought artists and architects from all over their empire and from its periphery (such as Ionian Greeks) to embellish their capitals Ecbatana and then Persepolis and Susa. The columned halls, or *Apadanas*, combined the Eastern love of grandeur and size with the Greek sense of proportion, and the virtuousity of elaborate stonemasonry with the tradition of massive architecture in brick. The door frames, the thresholds, the bases and the capitals of columns were made of stone and their decoration exalted the place of the Great King in the universe, at the side of mythical genii. The brick walls were decorated with colourful reliefs showing the imperial guard — the ''immortals'' extolled by Xenophon — keeping watch, flanked by winged monsters, over the security of the empire.

Alexander's conquest only substituted his empire for that of the Achaememids and, although it quickly became fragmented, the hellenistic East retained a large part of the splendour of the Persian court and its cosmopolitan culture.

Bowl decorated with a frieze of dogs
c 3600 BC
Hand made terracotta, painted —
diameter 12 cm
Susa, southwestern Iran, from a tomb
Excavated by J. de Morgan in 1897
Sb 3208

Hollow clay ball and clay tokens
for accounting
c 3300 BC
Unbaked clay — diameter 6.5 cm
Susa, southwestern Iran
Excavated by R. de Mecquenem
Sb 1927

Woman praying
c 3000 BC
Alabaster — height 11.8 cm
Susa, southwestern Iran
Excavated by R. de Mecquenem in 1909
Sb 69

Double vessel
c 2500 BC
Chlorite — length 18.3 cm
Susa, southwestern Iran
Excavated by R. de Mecquenem in 1909
Sb 2829

The Elamite goddess Narundi
c 2150 BC
Limestone — height 109 cm
Susa, southwestern Iran
Excavated by J. de Morgan in 1907
Sb 54

"Jar with the hoard"
c 2500-2400 BC
Terracotta, alabaster, copper from
Oman, stone — height of jar 51 cm
Susa, southwestern Iran, acropolis
Excavated by J. de Morgan in 1907
Sb 2723

Elamite god with golden hand
Elamite Period *c* 1800-1700 BC
Bronze and gold foil — height 17.5 cm
Susa, southwestern Iran
Excavated by R. de Mecquenem
Sb 2823

The "jar with the hoard" contained smaller earthenware jars and metal utensils, alabaster containers, cylinder seals and some jewels. This treasure probably represents the most valuable possessions of an individual. Some of the metal pieces, such as the sieve, have been proved by laboratory analysis to be made of bronze and are among the earliest examples of this alloy. The other metal objects are made of copper imported from Oman. The dishes of carved chlorite were a speciality of the peoples of Eastern Iran. The metropolis of Susa, strongly influenced by Sumerian civilization at this time, was at the centre of a trade network, and here these exotic products were redistributed.

Elamite funerary head
Elamite Period *c* 1500 BC
Unbaked clay, modelled and painted —
height 25.5 cm
Susa, southwestern Iran
Excavated by J. de Morgan, 1897-1912
Sb 2836

Sit Shamsi, rite to the rising sun
Elamite Period *c* 1150 BC
Bronze — length 60 cm
Susa, southwestern Iran, acropolis
Excavated by J. de Morgan 1904-1905
Sb 2743

*Cup on three feet in the form
of mountain goats*
Elamite Period *c* 1800 BC
Bitumen and limestone with
bronze nails —
height 28 cm
Susa, southwestern Iran
Excavated by R. de
Mecquenem in 1921
Sb 2737

Two men carrying offerings of goats
Elamite Period *c* 1150 BC
Gold and silver — height 6.3 cm
Susa, southwestern Iran
Excavated by J. de Morgan in 1904
Sb 2758 and 2759

Procession of Elamite warriors
Elamite Period *c* 1150 BC
Bronze — length 105 cm
Susa, southwestern Iran, acropolis
Excavated by J. de Morgan 1898-1900
Sb 133

Pendant in the form of a bull's head
Elamite Period *c* 1150 B
Lapis lazuli and gold — length 2 cm
Susa, southwestern Iran
Excavated by R. de Mecquenem in 1926
Sb 6589

Votive dove
Elamite Period *c* 1150 BC
Lapis lazuli with gold nails —
length 11.5 cm
Susa, southwestern Iran, acropolis
Excavated by J. de Morgan in 1904
Sb 2887

Toys — a hedgehog, a lion and a dove
Elamite Period *c* 1150 BC
Limestone and bitumen —
length 7.5 cm
Susa, southwestern Iran,
acropolis
Excavated by J. de Morgan
in 1904
Sb 2905, 2908 and 2909

Whetstone and rings with granulated decoration
Elamite Period *c* 1150 BC
Gold — diameter 2 cm
Susa, southwestern Iran, acropolis
Excavated by J. de Morgan in 1904
Sb 6657-6660

Bitumen is the first petroleum product to have been used by man. Sources in Mesopotamia and in southwestern Iran were exploited as early as the 5th millennium BC; the bitumen extracted was used as an adhesive, for caulking, for waterproofing and for other similar purposes. In Susa, there were artisans who specialized in making works of art of bitumen mastic, a composition also containing sand. From this they made cult stands, sculptures and dishes, which they exported to Mesopotamia. This prestigious craft, which flourished in the 3rd millennium BC, continued until the Neo-Elamite period, as seen in the charming relief of the spinner.

Elamite woman spinning
Neo-Elamite Period *c* 700-600 BC
Bitumen — width 13 cm
Susa, southwestern Iran
Excavated by J. de Morgan in 1897
Sb 2834

Vase handle in the form of a winged ibex
Achaemenid Period *c* 500 BC
Gold and silver — height 26.5 cm
Iran
Tyzskiewicz collection, acquired in 1898
AO 2748

Detail from the frieze of archers of the
Persian king's guard
Achaemenid Period *c* 500 BC
Polychrome glazed brick
height of the head 28 cm
Susa, southwestern Iran
Excavated by Marcel Dieulafoy in 1886
Sb 3302

When Darius the Great founded his capital at Persepolis, he did not neglect the old metropolis of Susa. The palace he built there combines two styles: the hypostyle halls with 20-meter-high columns are Iranian, the plan and the polychrome glazed brick friezes, on which the guard of the "immortals" is deployed, are Mesopotamian.

Achaemenid capital in the Persian style
from a column of the Apadana
Achaemenid Period *c* 500 BC
Limestone — height 320 cm
Susa, southwestern Iran
Excavated by Marcel Dieulafoy in 1886
AOD 1

Bowl decorated with a frieze of felines
c 3500 BC
Tepe Siyalk, Iranian plateau
Hand made terracotta, painted —
height 30 cm
Excavated by R. Ghirshman in 1933
AO 19447

Rein-ring decorated with a scene
of obeisance (detail)
c 2500 BC
Copper — height 18.4 cm
Luristan, western Iran
Acquired in 1931
AO 14056

Jug in the shape of a bull
c 1200-1100 BC
Burnished red terracotta —
length 36.5 cm
Azerbaijan, northwestern Iran
Given by M. Foroughi in 1962
AO 21112

*Mace-head decorated with a chariot
drawn by onagers*
c 2600 BC
Copper — height 13.4 cm
Luristan, western Iran
Gift of David-Weill family, 1972
AO 24792

Goblet decorated with mythological monsters
c 1200 BC
Electrum — height 11 cm
Northwestern Iran
Acquired in 1956
AO 20281

*Cheekpiece of horse-bit decorated
with a sphinx*
c 800-700 BC
Bronze — height 13.7 cm
Luristan, western Iran
Acquired in 1930
AO 12953

Dogs
c 2000-1800 BC
Silver — height 3 cm
Eastern Iran
Acquired in 1983
AO 28057 and 28058

D uring the Bronze Age there was a degree of cultural unity on the Iranian plateau because of the dissemination of commodities and ideas and the movement of people, from Mesopotamia in the west to Baluchistan in the east and the gates of Central Asia in the north-east. By tracing the dissemination of objects made of exotic stone, such as chlorite, carnelian and lapis lazuli, it is possible to establish the trade routes, which crossed through the great centres of trade, such as Susa. The female figurine made of chlorite and limestone in the workshops of Bactria is reminiscent of archaic Sumerian art both in style and in the use of materials of various colours. The silver dogs resemble objects from Tepe Hissar, in northern Iran, and from Quetta, in Baluchistan.

Female figurine
c 1800 BC
Chlorite and limestone —
height 17.3 cm
Eastern Iran
Acquired in 1969
AO 22918

From the 3rd century AD to the 7th, the Sasanian kings succeeded in uniting a very large part of the Near East. The Sasanians continued the Iranian traditions respected by the Persians, especially the preference for sumptuous objects. The silver vase decorated with graceful dancers in cut-out, applied gold foil displays Graeco-Roman influence: clinging drapery, fluttering veils, garlands. The mosaics that once decorated the palace at Bishapur also present scenes of the sophisticated life of an oriental court; the style in which the musicians are treated is taken from Greek art. This iconography continued in use, in the art of the Umayyads, for some time after the arrival of Islam.

Vase decorated with dancers
Sasanian Period *c* AD 350
Gold and silver — height 18 cm
Iran
Acquired in 1966
MAO 426

Harpist
Sasanian Period *c* AD 350
Mosaic — length 85 cm
Bishapur, Iran, palace of King Shahpur II
Excavated by R. Ghirshman
AO 26169

THE LEVANT AND
PRE-ISLAMIC ARABIA

The Levant

The Levant is more heterogeneous than any other part of the Near East: with a coastline on the eastern Mediterranean, it is susceptible to influences from the Aegean world and from Egypt. Divided into many political entities, it was always weak in the face of the ambitions of powerful neighbours: Egypt, Mesopotamia, Anatolia. Thanks to its position at the crossroads of the overland and maritime trade routes between all of these, it rejoiced in more or less constant prosperity, sustained by a flourishing agriculture and by the presence, in the mountains that follow the coastline, of good forests which furnished the timber that was in great demand in the entire Ancient Near East.

The Levant played a decisive part in the development of the first Neolithic communities. The trade in raw materials such as obsidian from Anatolia and then copper from Sinai were responsible for the prosperity of towns like Hacılar (in Anatolia), Jericho and Byblos.

Like Mesopotamia, the Levant had an urban civilization as early as the 3rd millennium BC. The pharaohs sent "presents" to Byblos, which controlled the trade in the cedars of Lebanon, in exchange for wood. The Egyptians saw affinities with their own divinities in those of the local pantheon; thus the "Lady of Byblos", goddess of the city, often took on the traits of the Egyptian Hathor.

During the 3rd millennium BC the Levant, together with Crete and continental Greece, witnessed the expansion of a palace culture whose centres were closely linked economically and diplomatically. From Knossos to Ugarit, from Mycenae to Enkomi in Cyprus and at Megiddo in Palestine, the grandeur of the palaces, of the houses and tombs of the aristocracy, bear witness to a spate of brilliant artistic activity. Caskets of polychrome Egyptian faience, gold drinking cups, cosmetic boxes, ivory toilet instruments, jewellery of carnelian and gold, alabaster vessels have all been found. They represent only a small part of the dowries of princesses or of the contents of the treasuries of the gods: what these would originally have included is known from contemporary lists. The cultivated elegance of these objects bears witness to an artistic lingua franca in which Egyptian, Cretan and Levantine elements are subtly blended.

The last half of the 2nd millennium was marked by the rivalry of Egypt and the Hittite empire for hegemony over the Levant; tablets in Babylonian cuneiform found in the Egyptian capital of El Amarna bring to life the rivalries that set the dynasties of Tyre, Ugarit, Byblos and Sidon against one another. The invasions of the "Sea Peoples" put an end to the palace civilization, in about 1200 BC.

From the 9th century BC onwards, the production of luxury goods resumed with the rise of the Phoenicians. The Phoenician cities sought markets and sources of raw materials overseas. At this time, Phoenician merchant ships took the place of those of the Mycenaean thalassocracy of the 2nd millennium, before they, in turn, gave way to the vessels of the Greeks, who took mastery of the seas at the end of the 7th century BC. The prophet Ezekiel, who lived at the time of the fall of Jerusalem in 587 BC, evoked the pride of Tyre at the height of its grandeur, comparing it to a ship whose mast were made from trees from Lebanon, whose sails were of Egyptian linen, whose purple tarpaulins came from the isles of Elisha and whose oarsmen came from Byblos, Arvad and Sidon.

The Phoenicians founded trading posts in Cyprus and, farther to the west,

Male figure
Chalcolithic Period *c* 3500-3000 BC Hippopotamus ivory — height 25 cm Safadi, Beersheba region, Negev Excavated by J. Perrot in 1958, gift of the Government of Israel
AO 21406

in Carthage, in Sicily and in Spain to which they were attracted by the gold of Tartessos. Carthage, originally a Phoenician colony, became a metropolis in its own right with its own Punic culture, which expanded during the 9th and 8th centuries BC, only later to be destroyed by the Romans.

The age of Assyrian imperialism and then the Neo-Babylonian conquest which entailed mass deportations to Babylon was a very unhappy time; to this time, however, the West owes a large part of its Mesopotamian heritage, which was assimilated by the exiles during the Babylonian Captivity and found its way into the Bible.

When he captured Babylon in 539, Cyrus the Great (559-530 BC) authorized the return of the exiles. The rule of the Persian kings was relatively peaceful despite serious revolts in Ionia and in Egypt; they kept the local dynasties in place and authorized them to mint coinages. They were tolerant of religious movements, permitting the reconstruction of sanctuaries, in particular the Temple in Jerusalem. Under the *Pax Persiana* a civilization open to hellenistic influence blossomed, particularly in Cyprus, Tyre and Sidon. In Cyprus, popular religion expressed itself in offerings of figures representing the votaries. Carved in a local limestone, these images display styles influenced by the art of various parts of the Mediterranean world: northern Syria, Ionia, Attica. The strangest manifestations of this cosmopolitan climate to be found on the mainland are surely the anthropoid sarcophagi: artists trained in the Greek tradition were commissioned by Phoenicians to carve mummy-shaped coffins, a concept of Egyptian origin, from the marble of the islands of Paros and Thasos.

The conquest of the area by Alexander the Great in 330 BC only accelerated the hellenization of the Syro-Palestinian littoral.

The history of the interior of Syria and of the heartlands of Anatolia were very different from that of the Syro-Palestinian coast. From the 6th millennium BC, the great Neolithic centres of Çatal Hüyük and Hacılar had sanctuaries decorated with paintings and sculptures that evoke fertility in the form of steatopygous "goddesses" giving birth. Matriarchal religions persisted until historic times. They are found in the Cappadocian towns that were engaged in the tin trade with Assyria: next to a group of cuneiform economic tablets, an administrative procedure borrowed from Mesopotamia, stone idols not very different from contemporary figurines found in Greece and the Cyclades, a manifestation of old indigenous traditions, were unearthed. During the 2nd millennium BC, the Hittite kingdom entered the ranks of the international powers by extending its rule over a part of the Syrian coastline and the Middle Euphrates region. The imperial ambitions of the Hittite kings, who designated themselves "My Sun", placed them in a state of rivalry with Egypt. The best known episode of that rivalry, the battle of Kadesh on the Orontes (c.1295 BC), was fought on the Egyptian side by Rameses II; the outcome was indecisive. The archives of the capital, Hattusas, near the modern village of Boghazköy, consist of tablets written in Babylonian cuneiform and others written in a new language and script, Hittite hieroglyphics. This form of writing survived the upheavals of the end of the Bronze Age that marked the end of the palace cultures of the Levant and the Aegean. The Hittite dynasty lost its ascendancy over the heartland of Anatolia but succeeded in maintaining a foothold in Carchemish on the Euphrates. From the 10th century BC on, the monumental architecture that evolved in the capitals of the small independent kingdoms of northern Syria, of the Syrian interior and of the Biblical land of Aram was embellished with powerful, spectacular basalt sculptures: sphinxes, lions and bulls guarded the gates and the walls were lined with orthostats decorated with mythological scenes. There are examples in the Louvre from Til-Barsip (Tell Ahmar), Zinjirli, Malatya and Marash. From the 8th century, however, this area was engulfed in the Assyrian empire and lost its artistic individuality.

Pre-Islamic Arabia

The Arabian peninsula and its periphery are culturally homogeneous, local differences notwithstanding. The languages and writing belong to two large families, Northwestern Arabic and Southern Arabic. There was, of course, strong cultural influence from the neighbouring areas, Mesopotamia and the Levant. Nonetheless, the common characteristics of this desert region, strewn with oases and traversed by transarabian caravan routes, permit the vast area that extends from the Yemen to Palmyra, from Petra and the Hauran to the Persian Gulf, to be considered as an entity. The early polytheistic religions of pre-Islamic Arabia, which were without idols, as well as the social organization based on the tribe, were also unifying factors.

The prehistory of Arabia is still not very well known. The best-known South Arabian kingdom of the 1st millennium BC is that of Saba, or Sheba, whose capital was Ma'rib. These kingdoms have been a source of fascination to Westerners throughout history, from Pliny the Elder to Rimbaud and Malraux.

They were situated in the *Arabia Felix* of the Greek geographers, in fertile valleys nestling in the well-watered mountains on the edges of the Wadi Hadramaut. Their economies were founded on agriculture and commerce; the remains of irrigation canals and dams, as well as many inscriptions commemorating public works intended to gather and distribute the water, have been found. The domestication of the camel made the development of trade over long distances possible. The oasis-dwellers set up a complex organization of overland caravans that tied in with the maritime trade: South Arabian inscriptions have been found in Egypt and even in the Greek islands.

South Arabian writing, which developed during the 1st millennium BC, conveys the character of the cultures and the art of this region: monumental and well-formed, displayed on public and religious buildings, on stelae privately dedicated to the gods or to the memory of the dead, on altars where incense was burned, the script has a place in the scheme of decoration as important as that devoted to figurative representation.

In the 1st century BC, a hellenized tribe that settled in the area around Petra founded the Nabataean kingdom; the Nabataeans were another people who amassed riches through the Arabian caravan trade. The façades of their rock-cut tombs, inspired by the hellenistic architecture of Alexandria and carved in the red sandstone of Petra, preserve the memory of a culture that combined Greek elements with those from Arabia. The conquest of the Levant by the Romans placed control of the Arabian trade in their hands, to their profit. In the 2nd century AD, it fell to Dura-Europos, founded by the Greeks at a staging post on the Euphrates, and above all to Palmyra, to dominate Eastern trade. Palmyrene merchants had agents along the length of the Euphrates and down to the entrance to the Persian Gulf; these agents equipped seafarers who went in search of silk, pearls and perfume from India in exchange for the purple dye and the glass of Phoenicia. Noble Palmyrene families embellished the city with colonnaded monuments and with statues; their tombs, whose towers stood beyond the ramparts, contained funerary portraits depicted with minute precision. They participate for all eternity at their own funerary banquets, with their jewels, their familiar implements, their clothes in the Greek or Persian style, the picture of a cosmopolitan society at the meeting point of East and West.

Worshipper and naked goddess
c 2300-2000 BC
Bronze — height 10 cm
Northern Syria
Acquired in 1898
AO 2736 and 2768

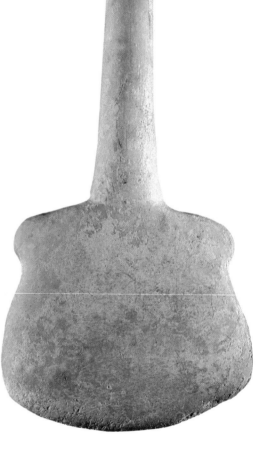

Schematic idol
c 2800 BC
Marble — height 16.2 cm
Yortan region, western Anatolia
Given by P. Gaudin in 1899
CA 1223.1

Rein-ring decorated with a figure of a man training
an equid
c 2500 BC
Copper — height 29.8 cm
Cappadocia
Chantre collection, deposited by the Musée Guimet in 1925
AO 9664

Hittite god
Old Hittite Kingdom *c* 1300 BC
Gold — height 3.8 cm
Yozgat, central Anatolia
Chantre collection, deposited by the
Musée Guimet in 1925
AO 9647

Votive plaque with engraved decoration
c 800-700 BC
Bronze — height 13.8 cm
Urartu, northeastern Anatolia
Acquired in 1976
AO 26086

Belt-buckle with granulated decoration
Orientalizing Period *c* 700 BC
Gold — height 8.5 cm
Aydin, western Anatolia
Acquired in 1886
AM 1853

U garit, now Ras Shamra on the Syrian coast, was
the capital of a flourishing kingdom in the 2nd
millennium BC. Its agricultural resources and its trade
links with both the Mediterranean world and the Euphrates provided the means for the development of a society based on palaces, with a sophisticated and luxurious
style of life and with a considerable literary output. There
are parallels in the mythological texts with Biblical
sources.

The storm-god Baal with a thunderbolt
Late Bronze Age *c* 1350-1250 BC
Sandstone — height 142 cm
Ugarit, north Syrian coast
Excavated by C. Schaeffer in 1929
AO 15775

Idol of the storm-god Baal
Late Bronze Age *c* 1350-1250 BC
Bronze and gold — height 17.9 cm
Minet el Beida, port of Ugarit, Syria
Excavated by C. Schaeffer in 1929
AO 11598

Cup with hunting scene
Late Bronze Age *c* 1250-1150 BC
Gold — diameter 18.8 cm
Ugarit, north Syrian coast, acropolis
Excavated by C. Schaeffer in 1933
AO 17208

Goblet decorated with the face of a goddess
Late Bronze Age *c* 1250-1150 BC
Polychrome Egyptian faience —
height 16.5 cm
Minet el Beida, port of Ugarit, Syria
Excavated by C. Schaeffer in 1932
AO 15725

"Mistress of the animals"
Late Bronze Age *c* 1200-1150 BC
Elephant ivory — diameter 13.7 cm
Tomb at Minet el Beida, port of
Ugarit, Syria
Excavated by C. Schaeffer in 1929
AO 11601

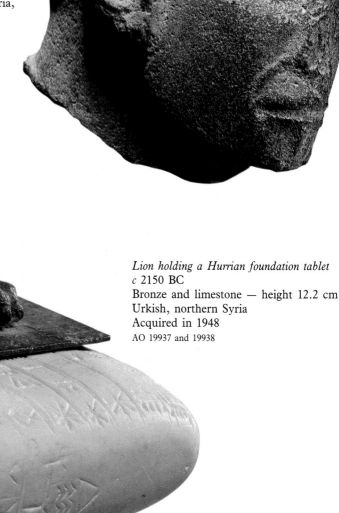

T he earliest historical documents that mention the
Hurrians are of the 3rd millennium BC and come
from northern Syria. The non-Semitic language in which
they are written was to be used in Syria and in Hittite
Anatolia. In the kingdoms of northern Syria, and especially in Carchemish, the language of the Hittites, written in a hieroglyphic script invented in the 2nd
millennium BC, survived the demise of the Hittite empire. In the 1st millennium, however, Aramaic, a local
West-Semitic dialect which was written in an alphabetic
script similar to Phoenician, gained the upper hand.

Head of a Syrian god
c 1700-1600 BC
Basalt — height 35 cm
Jabbul, northern Syria,
Acquired in 1926
AO 10831

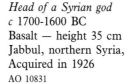

Lion holding a Hurrian foundation tablet
c 2150 BC
Bronze and limestone — height 12.2 cm
Urkish, northern Syria
Acquired in 1948
AO 19937 and 19938

Staghunt
Neo-Hittite Period, *c* 900 BC
Basalt — width 78 cm
Malatya, southwestern Anatolia
Acquired in 1891
AM 255

*Funerary stele of the Aramaean priest
Si-Gabbor*
c 650 BC
Basalt — height 95 cm
Neirab, Syria, Aleppo region
Acquired in 1897
AO 3027

Funerary stele of the scribe Tarhunpijas
Neo-Hittite Period *c* 800-700 BC
Basalt — height 74.5 cm
Marash, western Anatolia
Acquired in 1936
AO 19222

*Cup with figurative decoration: royal
victory and mythological battles*
c 750-700 BC
Silver gilt — height 17 cm
Idalion, Cyprus
Collection of the duke H. de Luynes,
acquired in 1853
AO 20134

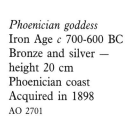

Phoenician goddess
Iron Age c 700-600 BC
Bronze and silver —
height 20 cm
Phoenician coast
Acquired in 1898
AO 2701

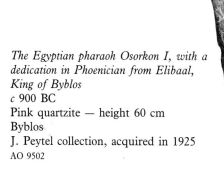

*The Egyptian pharaoh Osorkon I, with a
dedication in Phoenician from Elibaal,
King of Byblos*
c 900 BC
Pink quartzite — height 60 cm
Byblos
J. Peytel collection, acquired in 1925
AO 9502

Pectoral decorated with a falcon
c 1800-1700 BC
Gold — width 20.5 cm
Byblos, royal tomb I
Excavated by P. Montet in 1923
AO 9093

Winged genii
Assyrian Period *c* 750 BC
Ivory — height 8.5 cm
Arslan Tash, ancient Hadatu,
northern Syria
Excavated by F. Thureau-Dangin in 1929
AO 11465

Punic mask
c 400-300 BC
Terracotta — height 5 cm
Carthage, necropolis
Excavated by R.P. Delatre in 1901
AO 3783

Graeco-Phoenician sarcophagus
4th century AD
Basalt — height 65 cm
Tortosa necropolis, Phoenicia
E. Renan Mission, 1860
AO 4971

Graeco-Phoenician sarcophagus
Persian period *c* AD 500
Marble — length 210 cm
Arvad, Phoenician coast, Tripoli
region, necropolis
Pérétié collection, acquired *c* 1850
AO 4801

Moabite storm-god
c 1100 BC?
Basalt — height 103 cm
Shihan, ancient land of Moab,
Transjordan
Given by the duke H. de Luynes in 1856
AO 5055

Model of a shrine with sacred columns
Iron Age *c* 900 BC
Red terracotta — height 20.6 cm
Tell el Farah, Palestine
École Biblique Française excavations, 1954
AO 21689

"The Great Goddess" of Cyprus
c 500 BC
Limestone — height 98 cm
Tricomo, eastern coast of Cyprus
G. Colonna-Ceccaldi Mission, acquired
in 1870
N 3497

Priest with a bull's head headdress
Cypro-archaic Period c 530-520 BC
Limestone — height 43 cm
Golgoi, Cyprus
M. de Vogüé Mission, 1862
AM 2758

Ritual mask
Late Bronze Age c 1200-1150 BC
Terracotta — height 14.5 cm
Cyprus
Guimet collection, deposited in the Louvre
AO 22845

God banqueting
Late Bronze Age *c* 1200-1150 BC
Bronze — height 15.2 cm
Enkomi, eastern Cyprus
Excavated by C. Schaeffer in 1950
AM 2190 and 2191

Fertility figurine
Chalcolithic Period *c* 2200-2000 BC
Terracotta with incised decoration —
height 12.9 cm
Southwestern Cyprus
Couchoud Mission, 1903
AM 1176

Goddess or worshipper with raised arms
c 550 BC
Terracotta — height 43.5 cm
Karpas, eastern Cyprus
G. Colonna-Ceccaldi Mission,
acquired in 1872
MNB 319

Couple at a banquet
c AD 150
Limestone — height 57 cm
Tomb at Palmyra, Syria
Acquired in 1890
AO 2000

Triad of Palmyrene gods
c AD 150
Limestone — height 71 cm
Palmyra region, Syria
Acquired in 1957
AO 19801

*Statue of Amma'alay of the clan
of the Dharah'il*
c AD 150-200
Alabaster — height 45.5 cm
Yemen
Acquired in 1957
AO 20282

*Stele of Idjil: banquet and scene
of camel-raid*
c AD 150-250
Alabaster — height 55 cm
Yemen
Acquired in 1883
AO 1029

Lamp with handle in the form of an ibex
c AD 150-250
Bronze — height 21.5 cm
Aden
Given by P. Bardey in 1910
AO 4692

ISLAMIC ANTIQUITIES

The Early Centuries of Islam - 7th to 11th Centuries

After the death of Muhammad in Mecca in AD 632, the Arabs undertook a lightning conquest of the territories that had until then been dominated by Byzantium and the Sasanians. By 642, Syria-Palestine, Egypt and North Africa in the West, and Iran and Mesopotamia in the East had been vanquished. In the year 711, the armies of Islam set foot in Spain, Central Asia and India.

In 661 the centre of the empire moved from Arabia to Syria. The Umayyad dynasty (661-715) took Damascus for its capital, stabilized the power structure and continued to pursue territorial expansion. If, at an earlier time, Islamic art had borrowed craftsmen, techniques and a repertoire of decorative motifs from the old civilizations of the countries it had conquered, it very quickly acquired great originality. In this period architectural formulae were elaborated. The plan of the Dome of the Rock in Jerusalem (691), the earliest known Islamic religious monument, is reminiscent of that of the octagonal Roman martyria; however, the Great Mosque of Damascus (715) would, for centuries to come, provide the prototype for mosques built according to what has come to be known as the Arab plan. This plan is governed by the exigencies of religion and by the fact that prayer is oriented towards Mecca. This orientation *(qibla)* is indicated by a niche *(mihrab)* in the wall of the prayer hall. The naves are parallel to the *qibla* wall, and a transverse nave, wider and higher than the others and often enhanced by a dome, serves as a triumphal avenue to the *mihrab*. The prayer hall opens onto a courtyard surrounded by arcades, and several minarets complete the scheme. Nothing remains of the palaces of the caliphs of Damascus, but numerous ruined castles in the deserts of Syria, Iraq, Jordan and Palestine testify to the existence of centres of agriculture cultivated by ingenious methods for collecting water. The structure and decoration of these small forts display elements borrowed from both the Roman and the Sasanian traditions, but local elements are also present; a new type of dwelling resulted from this combination. The decoration is rich and imaginative and uses all the decorative techniques of late antiquity — such as stone sculpture, mosaic and mural painting — and of Iran, such as stucco. The all-over decoration is organized in a new way, divided geometrically into spaces that enclose intricate motifs. The Umayyad dynasty was overthrown in 750 as a result of a series of politico-religious uprisings.

With the Abbasids, the centre of the empire moved to Mesopotamia, which at that time was permeated with Iranian traditions. The Abbasids founded Baghdad, which very quickly became a great intellectual centre, a melting-pot where the philosophy, literature and science of the ancient world were translated, interpreted and advanced. In the realm of the arts, techniques diversified; some, whose secrets were jealously guarded, such as the procedure for applying metallic lustres to glass and ceramics, or the techniques for making opacified glazed wares were localized in the great urban centres. The number of fine objects known to have originated in large cities such as Samarra, Susa, Raqqa, Fostat and Cordoba is enough to prove the vitality of the arts from one end of the empire to the other.

The importance of trade, both overland and maritime, and the large number of Turkic mercenaries in the retinue of the caliph favoured a degree of Far Eastern influence. Although the empire broke up in the 9th century because it had become too large, and although in the 10th century the caliph, spiritual and temporal leader of the community, was faced with the rise of rival caliphates in Spain and in Egypt, art, for all its local variations, retained an overall unity in the general principles by which it was governed: the primacy of colour and

The archangel revealed to the prophet Muhammad — 8th surah of the Quran, page of the *Siyar-i Nabi*
1594-5
Gouache and gold on paper
height 37.5 cm; width 27.3 cm
Turkey
Acquired in 1984
Islamic section,
MAO 708

surface decoration over material, the taste for recurring all-over patterns and for geometric decoration, for stylization and for readily-apparent symmetry, the large-scale use of calligraphy and of themes reminiscent of princely pleasures.

Iran - 11th to 14th Centuries

Iran, with its ancient civilization and strong traditions in administration and in the arts, kept its language and its cultural heritage when it became largely Muslim; the ethic of the new conquerors was merely superimposed on these. The influence of Sasanian art persisted, underlying architectural and artistic achievements for a considerable part of the early centuries.

At the beginning of the 11th century Turkic nomads from Central Asia, who until then had been slaves within the Muslim world, penetrated into Iranian territory in large numbers. These same Saljuqs, who were Sunnis, reached Baghdad in 1055; there, they appointed themselves as protectors of the Abba-sid caliph, who recognized the title of "Sultan of the East and West" assu-med by their chief, Tugrul Beg. In 1070 a significant victory over the Byzantine emperor opened the gates of Anatolia to them. They established themselves in Iran and in Iraq while governors (atabeg) in their pay ruled in Syria and in Mesopotamia. After the death of the sultan Sanjar in 1157, the empire broke up into a large number of small communities, but the vigorous, original cul-ture — Iranian art invigorated by Asian elements — flourished until the Mon-gol invasion. These two centuries were distinguished by an intense intellectual life; one need only cite the names of the poets Firdawsi (941-1020) and Nizami (1141-1203), the theologian al-Ghazali (1058-1111) and the great physician and philosopher Ibn Sina (known in the West as Avicenna, 980-1037). The Sal-juqs brought the architecture they found on arrival in Iran, on which they conferred some new attributes, to the point of perfection. The buildings are of brick, faced with elaborate decorative brickwork or with glazed tiles or else they are decorated with stucco; the iwan (a large chamber open on one side) and the dome on pendentives are essential elements. In this period the plan with four iwans developed, for mosques — the Friday Mosque at Isfahan (1088) is the most beautiful example — and for the larger madrasas (theological col-leges) founded by Nizam al-Mulk, vizier of the sultan Malikshah. Funerary architecture may be divided into two types of mausoleum not very different from one another : the domed square chamber and the tomb tower. This was also a period of great artistic creativity in metalwork, ceramics and textiles. New techniques were developed, shapes and decorative motifs multiplied. In Khorassan, the metalworkers used more and more brass, at first with engra-ved, champlevé, répousse and openwork decoration, to which inlay in silver, red copper and gold were later added. From the middle of the 12th century, this decorative technique was in general use, and inlay, which at first consis-ted of wire, was elaborated to include finely engraved plaques.

At the beginning of the 13th century, the Saljuqs were supplanted by the Mongols, who shared their origins with the Saljuqs, but who were not yet con-verted to Islam and whose language was different. Led by Genghiz Khan, they conquered and founded the largest empire in the world. In 1258 Hulagu Khan put an end to the Abbasid caliphate in Baghdad, but his westward advance was finally stopped by the Egyptian Mamluks. On the death of Genghiz Khan the empire was split up into several "kingdoms", including that of the Yuan dynasty in China and that of the Il-Khans in Iran. After some years of stagna-tion in the cultural life of Iran there was a renewal. Several local dynasties, those of Tabriz, Shiraz and Isfahan among others, were patrons to a quite remar-kable development in the arts of the book, while in Kashan the techniques of making lustreware tiles to face large *mihrabs* as well as entire walls were handed down in secret from generation to generation of potters.

Egypt and Syria - 10th to 15th Centuries

In the 9th century, a great Shia upheaval disrupted the Near East. An imam of the Ishmaelite Shia sect who had been in hiding fled to North Africa; in Tunisia, claiming descent from Fatima, daughter of the prophet, he founded a caliphate which included Sicily. Wishing to supplant Baghdad, the Fatimids conquered Egypt in 969 and founded the city of Cairo. Thence they extended their dominion over Arabia and, for a time, over Syria. A brilliant civilization distinguished the two centuries of Fatimid rule. The development of an architecture enhanced by stone-faced walls with carved decoration and by elaborate portals may be studied from a number of mosques in Cairo whose dates are known. The mosque of al-Azhar (970-72) was established as a *madrasa* in 988, and thus became one of the first universities in the world. The art objects bear witness to the grandeur of the court and to the development of decoration: relatively abstract at first, massive and severe, still imbued with the influence of Mesopotamia, by the 12th century their decoration was figurative, picturesque and anecdotal, they were lighter and the treatment was altogether more delicate. There are wonderful examples of woodcarving and textiles, crafts traditionally associated with the Copts. Ceramics, mainly lustre wares, bear — unusually — the signatures of a great many potters. A considerable number of rock crystal and ivory carvings were brought to Europe at the time of the Crusades and the wooden ceiling of the Palatine Chapel (1140) in Palermo provides significant evidence of the painting of this period, of which only a few traces remain in Egypt and North Africa.

Between 1150 and 1163, the Fatimid viziers appealed to Nur al-Din ibn Zanki: ruler of Damascus and Aleppo, for help against the Crusaders. Nur al-Din sent General Shirkuh to Egypt; Shirkuh had himself appointed vizier. Salah al-Din ibn Ayyub (Saladin) succeeded him, put an end to the Fatimid caliphate, re-established the Sunni faith and founded the Ayyubid dynasty. In 1187 he succeeded in provisionally re-taking Jerusalem. Upholding the policies of his old master, Nur al-Din, he encouraged the economic prosperity accompanied by significant urban development and intense cultural activity that characterized the period in both Egypt and Syria. Imposing fortresses were built in cities such as Aleppo and Cairo and in strategic positions throughout the land. Numerous mosques and *madrasas*, the plans of which were gradually formalized, encouraged the diffusion of the Sunni faith. Portals of stone in courses of alternating colours, their vaults adorned with stalactites *(muqarnas)* and *mihrab* of polychrome marble embellish the austere stone architecture.

A great many decorative techniques were in use. From the end of the 12th century the art of enamelling and gilding glass was perfected in northern Syria. The arts of the book, especially, flourished; the manuscripts bear witness to influence from Byzantine Christian, Coptic and Syrian Monophysite prototypes and book decoration displays close links with that of such crafts as ceramics and metalwork. The symbolic evocation of nature in very simple terms throws into relief the realism and humour with which animals are rendered and the sharp sense of movement, narrative and dialogue in scenes in which people are represented.

In 1250, the Turkic slaves who formed the ruler's personal guard took over the reins of power. The Mamluks achieved victories over the Mongols and put an end to the Crusades in 1291. The Mamluk state, which was based on a strictly hierarchical military and administrative oligarchy, was a great power in the Mediterranean until 1517. Grand architectural complexes and spectacular tombs, whose somewhat ostentatious appearance reflects the craving for power of those who commissioned them, were built in Cairo in particular. Enamelled glass and metal inlayed with silver and gold reached their apogee at this time. Their decoration, enhanced with Far Eastern motifs borrowed from the Mongols, such as the lotus and the phoenix, display a predilection for inscriptions with tall uprights, often interspersed with coats of arms.

The Great Modern Empires

From the 15th to 16th centuries on, the Islamic world was divided into three large empires, often in a state of rivalry but nonetheless linked on the cultural level: the Ottoman Empire (1290-1922), the Safavid Empire (1501-1732) and the Mughal Empire (1526-1858).

The Ottoman Emirate of Anatolia, founded in the 13th century, quickly became a formidable power. After the conquest of Istanbul in 1453 by the Ottomans under Mehmet II (Fatih), the Ottoman dynasty, which adhered to the Sunni faith, was firmly established. At the time of Suleyman the Magnificent (1520-1560), the empire extended from Vienna to Morocco, surrounding the Mediterranean which had become in effect an Ottoman lake. The developments in architecture in Bursa and Edirne in the 15th century, and the influence of the architecture of Saint Sophia resulted in the elaboration of a central plan dominated by a large dome, each example of which is buttressed in a different way. Architecture in stone, championed by Sinan, was encouraged by the absolute and centralized power of the Ottomans, and by the palace where the imperial workshops were established. Among these workshops, pride of place was given to those of the painters, who designed the models that the craftsmen then adapted to suit the techniques of their crafts. Thus the style of the period was unified. Large motifs and brilliant colours confer a monumentality on the textiles woven in Bursa and Istanbul that is accentuated by the wide cut of of the caftans. The colours of the ceramic wares from Iznik evolved in the 16th century. First turquoise, then soft colours such as sage green and purple, and lastly, in the middle of the century, red, were added to the original blue and white.

After the downfall of Tamerlane's empire, the Safavid dynasty encouraged a degree of nationalism in Persia. The dynasty succeeded in containing the Ottoman advance on its territories and decreed the Shia faith the state religion. At the end of the 16th century, Shah Abbas built Isfahan, his new capital, on a grandiose scale, with large open spaces and gardens and with mosques that were entirely covered in predominantly blue tiles and which had high, bulbous domes. The decoration of the buildings and of the objects made at this time is highly refined and sophisticated. The small motifs are executed in delicate colours and references to nature and to literature are everywhere present. In the third quarter of the 16th century, first in Tabriz and then in Qazvin, the arts of the book reached an apogee. These are the achievements of a golden age centred on Isfahan. The fashion for large manuscripts declined in the 17th century, in favour of albums that included drawings, miniature paintings and calligraphy. From the end of the 17th century the style was modified by the effects of European influence.

Although the armies of the Muslims entered India as early as the 8th century, it was not until the 13th century that a stable presence was established. In 1526, after three centuries of sultanates at Delhi, Babar founded the Mughal Empire. An imposing architectural style developed in Delhi and in Agra; it was an adaptation of the Persian, reinterpreted in terms of local traditions in red sandstone highlighted with white marble at the time of Akbar, and later in white marble inlayed with semi-precious stones. Enormous tombs were built in formal gardens, the masterpieces of this genre being the mausoleum of the emperor Humayun (1565) and the Taj Mahal (1630). From the time of Akbar (1555-1605) an original style of miniature painting developed, born of the fusion of Persian and Indian traditions. The colours, simultaneously intense and delicate, accentuate the vigour of the animated compositions; the figures are portrayed as individuals, the details minutely studied and naturalism is in evidence. Art objects, much embellished with precious stones, share many of the characteristics of miniature painting.

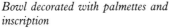

*Bowl decorated with palmettes and
inscription*
9th century to the beginning of the 10th
Earthenware with painted decoration
over an opaque glaze — diameter 19.6 cm
Mesopotamia
Alphonse Kann bequest, 1949
Islamic section, MAO 20

*Flagon decorated with simulated pleated
ribbons*
8th to 9th centuries
Blown glass with applied decoration —
height 13.5 cm
Susa, southwestern Iran
Susa excavations 1946-1948
Islamic section, MAO S 88

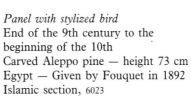

F rom the 8th century, potters in Mesopotamia
experimented with new techniques which they
quickly perfected, particularly that of making opacified
glazed wares and lustre wares. The decoration on the
former is painted over an opaque, generally white, glaze.
The colours used include green, brown and most of all
blue, obtained from the cobalt recently discovered in
Iran. Lustre decoration was achieved by applying metallic oxides to glazed and fired ceramics; during a second
firing in a reducing atmosphere the oxides were trans-
formed into fine films of pure metal.

Panel with stylized bird
End of the 9th century to the
beginning of the 10th
Carved Aleppo pine — height 73 cm
Egypt — Given by Fouquet in 1892
Islamic section, 6023

Bowl decorated with a ewer and a bouquet of palm leaves
10th to 11th centuries
Earthenware covered in slip with underglaze slip
decoration — diameter 34.5 cm
Nishapur, northeastern Iran,
or Samarkand
Gift of David-Weill family, 1950
Islamic section, MAO 95

Shroud of St Josse
Mid-10th century
Silk, samit — width 52 cm
length 94 cm
Khurasan, northeastern Iran
From a reliquary in the ancient Abbey
of Saint-Josse (Pas-de-Calais)
Islamic section, 7502

SPAIN

At the time of the Umayyad caliphate in Cordoba, the craft of ivory carving became highly refined in the workshops of the capital and of Madinat al-Zahra'; they produced cylindrical and rectangular boxes with an all-over decoration that evokes the pleasures of court life — hunting, music, banquets — but also makes use of old themes from the Near Eastern repertoire, such as confronted animals and birds in heraldic poses; it is deeply carved, with the details finely incised. The caskets (for jewels or for cosmetics?) have dedications, often dated, inscribed at the bottoms of their lids. They are dedicated to persons of high rank, often to princes — Al-Mughira was one of the sons of the caliph Abd-al-Rahman III, and assassinated in 976.

Lion with articulated tail
12th to 13th centuries
Cast and engraved bronze —
height 30.8 cm; length 54 cm
Spain
Bequest of Madame Louis Stern, 1926
Stern collection, Piot collection, Fortuny collection
(acquired by Fortuny in Palencia in 1872)
Islamic section, 7883

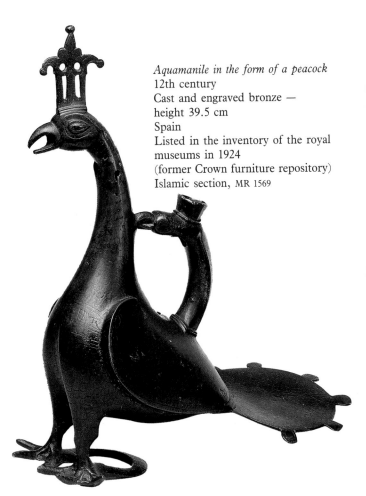

Aquamanile in the form of a peacock
12th century
Cast and engraved bronze —
height 39.5 cm
Spain
Listed in the inventory of the royal museums in 1924
(former Crown furniture repository)
Islamic section, MR 1569

Pyx inscribed with the name of al-Mughira
968
Carved ivory — height 15 cm;
diameter 8 cm
Cordoba
Acquired in 1898 — Riano collection
Islamic section, 4068

SALJUQ IRAN

In the 12th century the potters in the urban centres of Iran rediscovered the process for making vessels from siliceous clays. They sometimes mixed in crushed frit, thus making what was known in the West in the 8th century as soft paste porcelain. They emphasized the fineness of the wares with transparent patterns, made by introducing openwork into the vessels before applying the glaze; this predated the Chinese rice pattern technique. Some wares are decorated with motifs borrowed from the ornament in books, rendered in soft enamel overglaze colours and sometimes heightened with metallic lustre.

Bowl decorated with mounted falconer
End of the 12th century to the beginning of the 13th
Fritware with enamel colours, lustre and gilded decoration over an opaque glaze — diameter 22 cm
Kashan, central Iran
Acquired in 1970
Islamic section, MAO 440

Lion incense-burner
12th century
Cast bronze with pierced and engraved decoration, eyes inlayed with a turquoise-coloured material — height 28.2 cm; length 32 cm
Khurasan, northeastern Iran
Gift of David-Weill Family, 1933
Islamic section, AA 19

Bowl decorated with parrots
12th to 13th centuries
Fritware with pierced and incised
underglaze decoration — diameter 18.3 cm
Iran
Acquired in 1913
Islamic section, 6672

*Candlestick decorated with rosettes,
lions, hares and ducks*
End of the 12th century to
the beginning of the 13th
Hammered brass with repoussé
and chased decoration,
inlayed with silver and copper —
height 32.5 cm
Khurasan, northeastern Iran
Piet-Lataudrie bequest, 1909
Islamic section, 6315

*Ewer with the head of a cockerel and
waq-waq decoration*
Beginning of the 13th century
Fritware with underglaze painted
decoration
Kashan, central Iran
Given by the Friends of the Louvre
in 1970
Islamic section, MAO 442

IL-KHANID IRAN

The *Shahnama* — the Book of Kings — is the Iranian national epic; the best-known version is that written by Firdawsi in about the year 1000. This poem, which has about 60,000 couplets, recounts the battles of the Iranians and the Touranians, settled peoples against nomads, separated from one another by the River Oxus. One of the earliest extant illustrated examples was made in Tabriz in the middle of the 14th century. The illustrations, generally known to reflect Far Eastern influence, are tinged with lyricism, often dramatic, rapturously poetic but also very spirited.

Casket in the form of a mausoleum
14th century
Beaten brass with repoussé and chased
decoration, inlayed with engraved silver
and gold and with black composition —
height 24.2 cm
Fars, southwestern Iran
Acquired in 1893
Islamic section, 3355

Plate with fish roundel
End of the 13th century to the
beginning of the 14th
Fritware with enamel colours and gilded
decoration over an opaque glaze —
diameter 35.7 cm
Iran
Acquired in 1911
Islamic section, 6456

Wall panel
Second half of the 13th century
Fritware with painted and lustre
decoration over an opaque glaze —
height 78.5 cm; width 49.5 cm
Kashan, central Iran
Piet-Lataudrie bequest, 1909
Islamic section, 6319

The charge of the Faramarz horsemen,
page from a *Shahnama* by Firdawsi
Mid-14th century
Gouache and gold on paper —
height 40.5 cm
Tabriz, northwestern Iran
G. Marteau bequest, 1916 —
Demotte collection
Islamic section, 7095

FATIMID PERIOD

The exploits of the chase, like music, dancing and banqueting, always formed part of the iconography of princely life in the Islamic world. The perfect sport, it is also a manifestation of power and, furthermore, a symbol of the triumph of good over evil. If the dog is the indispensable companion of the hunt, two other creatures much used for this purpose were the falcon and the cheetah, very expensive animals whose training was a matter of great skill.

Cup decorated with an open flower
12th century
Fritware with lustre decoration over a
transparent glaze — diameter 19 cm;
height 8 cm
Northern Syria
Given by M. Despointes in 1845
Islamic section, LP 2463

Small plaques with scenes of recreation
12th century
Carved and painted ivory —
height 5.7 cm; length 29 cm
Egypt
Acquired in 1911 — V. Gay collection
Islamic section, 6265

Bowl decorated with a hare
12th century
Fritware with overglaze lustre decoration —
diameter 22.1 cm
Northern Syria
Léon Dru bequest, 1905
Islamic section, 6044

*Panel decorated with an antelope and
genre scenes*
11th century
Carved cypress wood — height 67 cm
Cairo, found on the site of the Fatimid
Western Palace at the time of its
demolition in 1874
Acquired in 1898 — Ambroise Baudry
collection
Islamic section, 4062

*Jar with the name of the sultan al-Malik
al-Nasir Salah al-Din Yusuf*
1237-60
Beaten brass with repoussé and chased
decoration, inlayed with engraved silver —
height 45 cm
Syria
Acquired in 1899 — Pope Urban VIII
Barberini collection
Islamic section, 4090

Apothecary jar
Beginning of the 14th century
Fritware covered in slip with
underglaze painted decoration —
height 32 cm
Egypt or Syria
Acquired in 1979
Islamic section, MAO 618

The tradition of making glass, at which the countries of the Eastern Mediterranean were the
supreme masters in antiquity, continued in the Islamic
period. In the 13th and 14th centuries the glassmakers
of Syria and Egypt brought the production of a dazzling
assortment of enamelled and gilded glass, in a great var-
iety of shapes, to perfection. The vessels are adorned with
figurative decoration inspired by book illustration, with
prayers for the patron who commissioned the piece written on the calligraphic borders and often with his coat
of arms. The bright colours accentuate the vigour of the
decoration.

Bowl decorated with a mounted archer
Beginning of the 13th century
Fritware with painted underglaze
decoration — diameter 20.7 cm
Northern Syria
Acquired in 1977 — Morin collection
Islamic section, MAO 610

Beaker with a frieze of horsemen
c 1260
Blown glass, enamelled and gilded —
height 15.5 cm
Northern Syria
Found in Orvieto *c* 1895 under the altar of a
destroyed church
Acquired in 1908
Islamic section, 6131

Door with two panels
End of the 13th century to the
beginning of the 14th
Rosewood inlayed with carved ivory
and ebony — height 164.2 cm
Egypt
Delort de Gléon bequest, 1914
Islamic section, 7462 (a + b)

85

Although they are found from the middle of the 12th century in Syria, coats of arms were used mainly during the Mamluk period both on monuments and on objects, mainly in the 13th and 14th centuries. They take the form of symbols — fleurs de lys or crescents, for example — insignias of office — such as swords, trumpets or chalices — animals — such as panthers and eagles — *tamgha* (Turkish tribal signs), or inscriptions giving the name and titles of the sultan. The coat of arms of a specific emir may incorporate several elements: that of Tuguztimur, a high dignitary who ended his career as viceroy of Syria, reflects his office of chief cup-bearer and his membership of the house of the sultan Nasr al-Din Muhammad ibn Qala'un, whose emblem is the eagle.

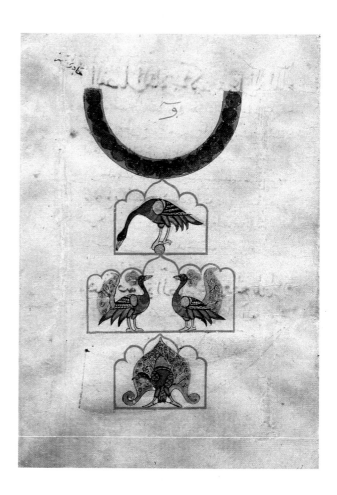

Clock with peacocks, page of the *The Book of Knowledge of Ingenious Mechanical Devices*, by al-Jazari
1354
Gouache on paper embellished with gold and silver — height 40 cm
Egypt or Syria
Given by E. Mutiaux in 1926
Islamic section, 7875

Mosque lamp
Mid-14th century
Blown glass with enamelled and gilded decoration — height 27 cm
Syria or Egypt
Davillier bequest, 1885
Islamic section, 3110b

Carpet with geometric decoration
Beginning of the 16th century
Wool, asymmetrical Persian knot — length 173 cm; width 125 cm
Cairo
Given by Godefroi Brauer, 1921
Islamic section, 7382

Basin known as the "Baptistery of Saint Louis"
Beginning of the 14th century
Beaten brass with chased decoration and
inlays of silver, gold and black composition
Former treasury of the chapel of the
Château de Vincennes
Islamic section, LP 16

Bottle with the arms of Tuquztimur
c 1345
Blown glass, enamelled and gilded —
height 50.5 cm
Syria or Egypt
Acquired in 1893 — Spitzer collection
Islamic section, 3365

OTTOMAN TURKEY

I n the 16th century, the directions that art was taking were guided by the imperial workshops, particularly by those of the painters, in Istanbul. The designs were transmitted to men working in other crafts, a system that conferred considerable unity of decorative style on luxury articles of all sorts. In about 1530, the painter Sahkulu was acclaimed for creating the ''saz'' style, which became immensely popular. Large compositions of long, supple, curving leaves with jagged edges, combined with half-rosettes and flowers in full bloom, cover the entire surface of an object.

Jar in the shape of a mosque lamp
decorated with arabesques
c 1515
Fritware with decoration painted over a
slip and under a lead glaze —
height 33.2 cm
Iznik, Turkey
Acquired in 1902
Islamic section, 5547

Peacock perched among flowers
c 1550-55
Fritware with decoration painted over a
slip and under a lead glaze —
diameter 37.5 cm
Iznik, Turkey
R. Koechlin bequest, 1932
Islamic section, K 3449

*Tympanum from the Mosque of Piyale
Pasha in Istanbul*
c 1573
Fritware with decoration painted over a
slip and under a lead glaze —
height 70 cm; width 136 cm
Iznik, Turkey
Given by G. Bapst in 1889
Islamic section, 7509

Dish with arabesque and lotus decoration
Mid-16th century
Hammered silver with engraved,
chased and stamped decoration —
height 3.4 cm; diameter 12.4 cm
Istanbul
Given by the Friends of the Louvre in 1990
Islamic section, MAO 850

Tankard with "four-flower" decoration
c 1565-75
Fritware with decoration painted over a
slip and under a lead glaze —
height 27.5 cm
Iznik, Turkey
Piet-Lataudrie bequest, 1909
Islamic section, 6323

SAVAFID AND QAJAR IRAN

Until the 15th century, the large number of pictures of rulers that were painted were more in the nature of symbolic representations than true portraits. One of the first known portraits is that of Mehmet II (Fatih), who conquered Constantinople in 1453; the work of a Turkish artist, in terms of resemblance it is in no way inferior to those of Bellini and the Italian medal-makers of the period. The art of portraiture flourished in the following centuries in the Ottoman empire as well as in Persia and in Mughal India. Although the poses are often conventional, the accent is placed on the face and on details of dress.

Scenes of rustic life — signed
Muhammadi
1578
Drawing enhanced with colours and
gold and silver on paper —
height 39.4 cm; width 26.3 cm
Tabriz or Qazvin, Iran
G. Marteau bequest, 1916
Islamic section, 7111

Princely reception in a garden
End of the 16th century
Gouache and gold on bristolboard —
height 38.6 cm; width 24 cm
Iran or Transoxiana
G. Marteau bequest, 1916
Islamic section, 7100a

Carpet decorated with animals
16th century
Silk, asymmetrical Persian knot —
height 124 cm; width 109 cm
Kashan, central Iran
Given by J. Peytel in 1914
Islamic section, 6741

*Portrait of Shah Abbas I with one of
his pages*
Signed Muhammad Qasim
10th February, 1627
Drawing enhanced with colours and
gold and silver on paper —
height 27.5 cm; width 16.8 cm
Isfahan, central Iran
Acquired in 1975
Islamic section, MAO 494

Kilim decorated with literary themes
End of the 16th century to the
beginning of the 17th
Silk and silver thread —
length 249 cm; width 139 cm
Kashan, central Iran
Given by Doisteau in 1904
Islamic section, 5946

Black iris — signed Muhammad Hadi
End of the 18th century
Gouache, watercolour and gold on
paper — height 26.5 cm
Shiraz, southwestern Iran
Acquired in 1987
Islamic section, MAO 791

*Bottle decorated with animals in a
landscape*
17th century
Earthenware with lustre decoration
over a transparent glaze — height 31 cm
Iran
Acquired in 1893
Islamic section, 3373

Portrait of 'Alidja Muqarrib al-Kaqan Dust'ali Han, signed Mirza Baba al-Husayni al-Imami
1846
Gouache on paper —
height 39.3 cm; width 25.4 cm
Tehran
Acquired in 1987
Islamic section, MAO 774

Narghile base decorated with garlands
17th century
Fritware with underglaze painted decoration — height 28 cm
Iran
Acquired in 1982
Islamic section, MAO 688

Small bowl with flowered decoration in arched panels
17th century
Fritware with underglaze painted decoration — diameter 11.6 cm;
height 8.5 cm
Kirman(?), eastern Iran
Acquired in 1983
Islamic section, MAO 700

Page of calligraphy
16th century (calligraphy);
17th century (margins)
Ink, gouache and gold on paper
Iran (calligraphy) and India (margins)
G. Marteau bequest, 1916
Islamic section, 7157

MOGHUL INDIA

P ainting at the court of the Great Mughal was characterized in the 17th century by minute attention
to detail in the rendering of nature and portraits. The
faces are treated with great discernment and dress, jewellery and weapons are drawn with such attention to detail
that the paintings may be dated by comparison with the
actual objects depicted. The balance of the compositions
and the stylization of certain motifs throw into relief the
naturalism with which the animals and plants are treated, their essential characteristics caught by the artists.

Narghile base
18th century
Blown glass, enamelled and gilded —
height 16.5 cm
Mughal India
Acquired in 1985
Islamic section, MAO 739

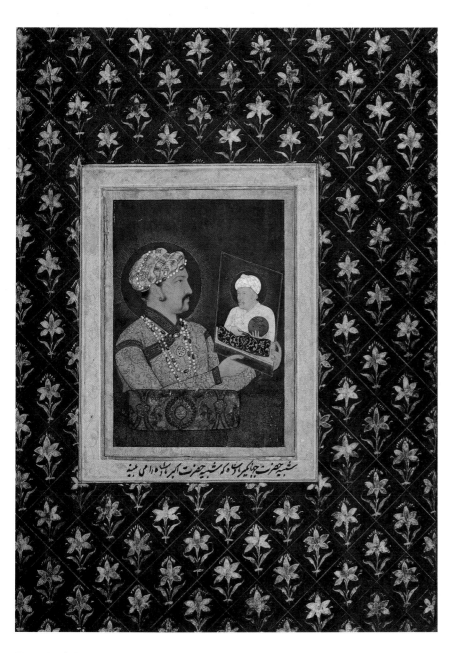

*Portrait of the emperor Jahangir
(1569-1627) holding a portrait of his
father Akbar (1542-1605)*
Beginning of the 17th century
Watercolour and gouache on paper,
enhanced with gold —
height 12 cm; width 8.3 cm
India
Acquired in 1894
Islamic section, 3676 B

Dagger with horse's head handle
17th century
Damascened damask steel, engraved
jade inlayed with gold and precious
stones — length 50.5 cm
Mughal India
Acquired in 1927 — Salomon de
Rothschild collection
Islamic section, 7891

Fragment of the tympanum of a window
12th to 13th centuries
Carved volcanic stone — radius 46 cm
Caucasus, Daghestan
Acquired in 1938
Islamic section, AA 266

Photograph credits : Scala Publications Ltd.
Réunion des Musées Nationaux (12, 19hd, 20hd, 20b, 21g, 21b, 22bg,
22bd, 25, 26g, 27, 28g, 29, 30b, 33g, 34, 39bg, 39bd, 40hg, 41,
42hd, 42b, 46, 47, 48, 50b, 51b, 52, 57hg, 58g, 59, 62g, 62b, 63h,
67bd, 68, 69hd, 69bd, 70, 74, 75, 76, 77, 78, 79, 80, 81, 82, 83,
84, 85, 86, 87, 88, 89, 90, 91, 92, 93, 94, 95, 96)

Designer : Jérôme Faucheux

Printed in Italy by Graphicom
Typeset by Intégral Concept
Origination by Charente Photogravure
Photos Hubert Josse
Dépôt légal : octobre 1991